The Battle
of Anzio

The Battle of Anzio

T. R. Fehrenbach

OPEN ROAD
INTEGRATED MEDIA
NEW YORK

ISBN 978-1-4976-3733-7

This edition published in 2014 by Open Road Integrated Media, Inc.
345 Hudson Street
New York, NY 10014
www.openroadmedia.com

Foreword

THE BATTLE OF ANZIO is a realistic narrative account of a great battle. It is based on a combination of official historical documents and the personal experiences of men who fought there, obtained through interview Major Fehrenbach has shown events as they happened, from field Army level through corps, regiment and platoon, down to the ultimate unit in war—the individual fighting man.

Nothing is inevitable in war. A battle is never over until the last gun has sounded. When it has, it was not the caliber of the guns which was important but the caliber of the men who held them.

Clausewitz wrote: "Although techniques change daily, tactics never change." Nor does the fact that man is the most important factor in war change. Nations which in the past have placed their faith in hardware and secret techniques have found they stored up treasures for moth and rust.

When we write of battles, we write of men. Whatever weapons systems we use, let us never forget that the unchanging ingredient of victory is still the individual fighting man. This has been true of our history. It will be true of our future.

THE BATTLE OF ANZIO shows both the agony of command decisions and the heroism of men who carry them out.

WILLIAM H. SIMPSON
General, United States Army Retired

Author's Preface

Shortly after the fighting ended in Europe in World War II, the Allied troops held a big victory parade. The bands blazed; the flags went by. Then the troops marched. The veterans of Anders' Polish Corps had tears in their eyes: they knew Poland would exist again. The French officers came erect, the *mystique* of the French Army in their faces: the honor of France was avenged. And as the bagpipes wailed, the quiet, dogged look on British faces told how they had lived their finest hour.

In the American marching units someone shouted, "Let's get this damn thing over with and go home!"

Unless you understand that shout immediately, you can never undestand the American GI in World War II. For the Americans who brought either a professional attitude or an ax to grind to the European war were not representative of the majority of us. For in our hearts, no matter what we were told, we never believed our existence as a nation was remotely endangered. We knew merely that there was a dirty job, and it looked like we were the ones to do it.

It is to our everlasting credit that, feeling as we did, we did it so well. Every other army, at some time or another, was defending its own soil. But we were able to match their every effort because we had the pride of free men, the pride in being Americans—and when at last we were in a tight spot—and often not until that moment—we were unbeatable. This is an inner toughness you cannot instill with propaganda of fine phrases. Either a people has it or it has not.

So long as we have it, no matter what we proclaim or do not say, or how inept or weak our leaders, we shall continue to survive. Because God help those who back Americans into a corner. It is then, when others give up, that we show what we can do.

We do what has to be done. That is a phrase we could put on our battle standards. We have no Wagnerian sense of grandeur; we have an imperfect sense of history. None of us believe death on the battlefield is particularly desirable. We seldom hate our enemies, even while they are killing us. But what has to be done, we do!

But when the guns are stilled, and the battle honors placed upon our flags, what are the names that touch our hearts? Do we remember the terrible slaughter of our foes, the forcing of our national will on others, the heady draughts from the cup of total victory?

What we recall are not the great victories, but the bad times, the days that tried our souls. Valley Forge. The Alamo. Bastogne. Pork Chop Hill. Anzio. On many of these fields we did not win. But we remember that our spirit triumphed, regardless of to whom history assigns the victory.

This book is about the Anzio beachhead, from ill-starred beginning to triumphant ending. Who won, who lost, which general was right, which mistaken, no longer seems important. What is important is for us, once again, in understanding, deep pride and deeper humility, to know the story of the dogface soldier.

T.R.F.

Acknowledgments

The big picture of what happened at Anzio is in the official records, the division histories, the diaries and post mortems of the generals. But most of these pages are antiseptic—the agony and controversy of Anzio are badly strained, and too little of the feeling comes through.

While documents are vital to understanding, personal experience alone gives us the true flavor of battle, of victory or defeat. In these chapters are revealed men who were sensitive or stolid, men who were wholly brave, men who knew normal fear, and men who cracked under pressure. They were also men who were wounded, captured, evacuated or who went through the worst of it without a scratch.

Each of these stories is a part of Anzio, without which the whole is imperfect.

When I first began taking down these narratives, a former divisional operations officer told me: "This was fifteen years ago. I am bound to have some of it wrong. Besides, I never knew exactly what was happening, anyway." There will be errors in these narratives. This is to be expected. Sometimes the accounts contradict. One man vividly remembers a rose garden; a man who was beside him says it was a vineyard. War is like that. A man, to survive, can only focus his mind on what is immediately before him. He does not worry too much about how he got on the battlefield—when a man is under fire, there is no time to think of great ideals, or the idiocies of politicians.

Men remember the irrelevancies; these chapters are sprinkled with them. It is sometimes the irrelevancies, like the fear of catching cold, or the longing for beer, that reveal the human heart and soul. From irrelevancies, the truth often seeps through.

Where the narratives would invade privacy, or otherwise embarrass the narrator, names have been changed. No man likes to have recorded that he shot another in the back, or told his men not to bother taking prisoners. In some cases, descriptions and circumstances have been slightly altered also, to protect the individual.

An occasional liberty has been taken to keep the narrative tight: for example, Hitler did not confer with Kesselring and Rommel at the same time. But what was said remains the same, and from it Hitler made his historic decision.

The major command decisions at Anzio—General Lucas' not to drive on the Colli Laziali, and General Clark's to shift the attack toward Rome to the north-west—are history. They will be discussed and argued for many years to come, but they have been fully documented.

Some men, reading this, will see a name they know. Most will not. For the names are not important.

After all, not far from where this is being written, there rises a cenotaph bearing the names of the men who died in the Alamo. Though thousands pass it each day, only a handful of people know more than a few of those names. But everyone knows what those men did before they died.

That is the important thing.

T. R. F.

The Casualty List for Anzio
(Allied Forces)
Killed in Action: 7,000
Wounded in Action or Missing: 36,000.
Hospitalized for Sickness or Injury: 44,000

Table of Contents

The Battle of Anzio
January 22, 1944—June 1, 1944

Part One
Beachhead

Part Two
Bloodletting

Part Three
Breakout

Part One

Beachhead

In the fall of 1943, after years of victories, the Axis had fallen back, been forced on the defensive. In Tunisia and at Stalingrad, Hitler had lost the flower of his land armies. The Allies had stormed ashore at Salerno in southern Italy, knocking the Italian Government out of the war. But the Wehrmacht still had teeth. Salerno had been a near-disaster, although it ended in victory. The memory of near-defeat remained, to give the Allied generals pause.

Now, however, the top Allied strategists saw that they had closed the ring; the Axis was encircled, its strategic defeat assured. Men began to talk of victory, an early finish to the European holocaust.

On the ground in Italy, the soldiers who were engaged with the Wehrmacht, who would do the future fighting to accomplish victory, were not talking. No one knew better than they that they were locked in bitter battle with a wily, numerous and well-equipped foe, who could hardly be considered defeated.

Strategic encirclement is one thing; final victory on the ground is another. The latter is never bought cheaply; whether in the days of Caesar's legions or in the atomic age, each foot of ground brings its price.

In Italy, some of the bloodiest fighting of this or any war had just begun.

1

"Hit the Beach!"

"It will astonish the world. . . ."—*Winston Churchill, referring to the assault landings at Anzio, January 22, 1944*

What a night for a boat ride, Lieutenant Louis Martin thought. The sky was clear, showing a million stars, and the air balmy, warm for winter even on the southern Italian coast. The waters of the Tyrrhenian Sea, one of the world's loveliest, were still, hardly rocking the circling LCIs. Thank God for that, Louie Martin thought; it was bad enough going up on a hostile beach without being seasick!

He stood up in the front of the landing craft, trying to see in to Yellow Beach, between the towns of Anzio and Nettuno. He thought he saw the white gleam of gentle breakers on the shore, against the brooding dark background of the town of Anzio and the bluff above it. He wiped spray from his thick glasses, reaching instinctively for his spare set.

Damn it, he had forgotten them—and with eyes like his, that wasn't good. If he'd had the dough, he'd have bought some of those new things, those contact lenses, before he left the States in '42. Then he wouldn't have to squint and cheat and memorize the eye chart every time he had a physical.

1

He grinned. A damn good thing he wasn't in the Navy. They didn't just let you read off a Snellen chart; they put some kind of instrument in your eyes and made sure. Louie Martin couldn't have got a commission in the bloody Navy, which was one reason he was in Darby's Rangers.

As for the other reasons, he was going to see a damned psychiatrist after the war. If he lived that long. He raised a thin-forearm before his face, trying to read the dial of his ordnance watch in the luminous reflection of the LCI's wake. He said out loud, "0150, fellows. H-Hour is 0200. About time for the Navy to start shooting."

He looked at the darkened faces to either side of him, and at the shapeless men huddled behind him in the landing craft. He grinned again. "What's the matter? Aren't you enjoying it? Here Task Force 81 is providing you a scenic tour and the boat ride, all at great expense—"

A couple of the faces grinned back at him. Henry, a short, dark, belligerent soul, had his long knife out of his boot, sharpening it against the leather.

Pella, the Italian kid, his face tight, said, "Put that goddamn thing away, Henry. You give me the creeps. You ain't gonna get close enough to a Kraut to stick him, anyway—"

The short man flared, "I'll put it up your ass if you don't shut your yap."

Private Pella moved, trying to struggle to his feet. Louie Martin gave him a firm shove on the shoulder. "Hold it. After we take Anzio, you can tear each other up. Not now!"

Pella sank back, and Henry slowly put the knife away. Lieutenant Martin was a skinny, four-eyed kid himself, but when he spoke, his men listened. He had that quality. No one who did not could not be a Ranger officer.

He looked back in the boat to his platoon sergeant. Krueger regarded him sourly, without expression. Krueger was never a happy sort, but he was steady, and the kind of balance wheel these charged-up Rangers needed.

"Take it easy, you guys," Krueger said.

Like Martin, he understood how the tension built up before you hit the beach. The men got tighter and tighter, until finally they had to explode. That was a good thing—if they exploded against the Germans.

Rangers were "special"troops—call them an elite, if you must. But they were human, too, and they got just as nervous as anyone else going in on these beaches—as nervous as the boys of the veteran 3rd Division, attacking over Red and Green Beaches to the South, or the Limey 1 Division and the Commandos of Force Peter, going in north of Anzio.

The main way the Rangers and those hopheads in the 509th Parachute Battalion, going in beside them to seize Anzio's sister town of Nettuno, were different was that they volunteered for jobs like this. When you volunteered for the Ranger Force or the paratroops, you were asking for trouble and, by God, you found it, Martin thought.

2

What had that doc told him back in Sicily? "A sane man doesn't look for danger; if he's normally brave, he just tries to meet it when it comes."

And here he was, a nut leading a platoon of nuts, all trying, like the touchy Henry or the nervous kid, Pella, or the Jewish boy from New York—Meyer—to prove something. Martin shook his head, shifting his carbine. Hell, no, it was more than that. A lot of the men in the Ranger battalions just liked to fight. Some of them, like himself, just had to be in the front of it. Put it all together, with the toughest training in the world, and you had one of the best damn fighting units the U.S. Army had ever seen!

And Louie Martin was looking at the dark, shadowy shore, not with fear, but with a deep excitement in his veins. Why the hell didn't the Navy open up?

Then the darkness was streaked with red fire. Rockets whooshed up from the landing craft and Navy vessels all over Anzio Bay. The flaring trials arced, hissing over the still water, and the beaches rocked with the impact of multiple explosions. *Boom-boom-boom,* the sound echoed back across the waves to Martin's ears. He straightened up, looked toward Yellow Beach, directly between Anzio and Nettuno, where his own LCI would beach itself. Great gouts rose in the water, and further inland, as the beach itself and the dark buildings behind it were splashed with fire and flying metal.

"That'll wake the Krauts up," he said aloud, with satisfaction.

Boom-boom-boom-whoom!! The sky off to the right and south flared with fiery brilliance. Over there General Lucian Truscott was sending all three regiments of his 3rd Division ashore in the first wave. The Limeys must be firing up north, too, but to hell with them. Louie Martin had enough to worry about right here. The gobs had pointed the LCI straight in now, and its great engines were roaring. On both sides, other LCIs and the bigger boats, the LSTs and slim LSI, were streaming toward the shore. *Whoosk-whoosh-whoosk! Bam-Bam-Bam!*

"How long they gonna shoot up the beaches?" Private Henry asked sullenly.

"Ten minutes," Martin said quietly. He was thinking, back there on the cruiser *Biscayne,* Major General John P. Lucas' flagship, the war correspondents were probably having their first cup of coffee and getting ready to write: "Anzio, Italy, January 22, 1944. This morning at 0200, VI Corps, more than 50,000 strong, landed sixty miles behind the German lines in Italy. General Mark W. Clark, of whose Fifth U.S. Army the VI Corps is a part, in briefing war correspondents called this operation a *calculated risk. . . .*"

Louie Martin stopped musing. When the brass used that term, chum, look out! He watched the approaching shore, feeling an urgent desire to urinate. That was silly, a part of his mind told him; he couldn't go if he had the time.

Somebody behind him snapped a rifle bolt, and he turned, said sharply, "Watch it! Let's not have anybody shot in the boat!"

3

He shook his head, remembering the soft, Carolina voice of his battalion commander, Jack Dobson. "Fifth Army, with the 36th Texas Division, is going to attack across the Rapido on the Cassino front. What we do is an end run, up the Italian west coast to hit the Krauts in the flank while the 36th's keeping them busy. We land at this little resort town, Anzio, with General Penney's British 1 Div., and Truscott's 3rd. The 45th and the 1st Armored will come in later to back us up. The idea is, once we've secured a beachhead, we move inland to the Alban Hills south of Rome and blow a fat hole in the Krauts' communications. With any luck, we'll link up with the rest of Fifth Army in a few days. The Rangers' job is simple: we take and clear out the town of Anzio itself."

The other officers had smiled at that. Street fighting was a nasty business any time. But the Rangers, like the British Special Forces, or Commandos, were especially trained for it. In fact, the Rangers had been modeled on the British forces—companies of three officers and sixty-three EMs, six companies and a HQ company in a battalion, or about 470 in all. This was almost identical to a British Commando, or Special Forces, battalion. Only the name was different. No one wanted to use the term "Commando"for American forces; the glory of that name would be for all time British.

In North Ireland, in 1942, General Truscott, who was then attached to the staff of the Commander of Combined Operations and had helped form the new American forces, had selected the name "Ranger." There was no more honorable name in American military history.

Boam-Boom-boom-pow! The explosions and bright flashes were close ahead now, and the LCI streamed forward. Crouching, Martin looked for the purple-orange winks of machine-gun fire from the beach, listened for the long rip of the MG 42s. But the beach was quiet except for the rocket barrage. Maybe the Krauts were going to play it like the Japs, let the first wave come ashore before they opened up. Where the hell were they—in bed?

Then, suddenly, a battery blazed from the shore. A heavy shell passed over the LCI with a shriek, while the helmeted heads rippled like grain, ducking down. The shore gun fired again, and a spout of water burst high off their stern. But guns of the big cruisers offshore were swinging now, vomiting flame.

Whirrrrr. The shells roared over like express trains, bothering the Rangers worse than the wild German fire. *Brrroom-broom!* Flame spouted high back of the beaches, and the enemy guns went dead.

Louie Martin kept thinking, *Hit the beach, move back from the water. Then we flank Anzio itself and take it, house to house, if necessary.* He was trying to remember the maps and diagrams of the town with which he had briefed his men. My God, his mind was blank. All he could remember was that Anzio was a Roman beach resort, in the old days.

He lifted up, still surprised that no small-arms fire sang against the LCI.

4

He could see the beach plainly now in the clear night. There was a long waterfront street up from the beach, and a dark mass of stone buildings behind that. Way back a heavy blackness rose; that must be the bluff on the maps. Now Louie had it—he recalled Anzio-Nettuno was really almost one town, stretched along the seacoast.

The towns covered about three miles, but they only went back a block or two from the water. Sure, everybody wanted a sea view, just like back home. And the buildings were villas and four-and five-story apartments where the rich Eyeties came for the summer, and office buildings, too. Everything was of stone, like all over Italy, and would be bloody hell to reduce if defended.

He looked behind him, shouted, "Lock and load!"

The weapon bolts clattered, and blackened faces drew back from white teeth. Even Pella was straining forward now, ready to dash up the beach. Martin heard Krueger shout, "Don't linger in the boat!"

By God, Martin thought, Bill Darby would be proud, no matter what happened in Anzio. The colonel was only class of '33 at West Point, a young man, not much past thirty. But Louie Martin found it hard to think of Darby as a West Pointer. Sure, he was erect, keen, intelligent, afire with enthusiam and the old school try—but he didn't play war by the book either. The rules didn't always work, and Bill Darby knew it, where a lot of his classmates at that general factory didn't.

The high brass was dubious of the Rangers. It was the same all over. The British brass didn't like Stirling's Commandos either. The professionals always distrusted anybody who didn't fight by the book.

Hell, even that Kraut, Skorzeny, probably had trouble with the *Junker* generals. He was head of the Kraut Commandos, and he was still only a captain! Nobody really liked elite or special troops. The generals distrusted them, and the dogfaces hated anybody who thought they were hot stuff.

I don't blame the dogfaces, Martin thought; *we cop the headlines, like the damn Marines.* He smiled. Then, as he loaded his carbine, with the small part of him that thought like an officer, he agreed a little with the brass. Outfits like the Commandos or Rangers drew tough men, sure, but they also drew the trouble seekers. And men who sought danger and death like thirsty men wine— well, they didn't take to discipline, sometimes. A general would rather lose a war than lose discipline.

But when a special and dirty job was there to be done . . . Louie Martin straightened his glasses on his thin nose, shifted his carbine. He realized the Navy rocket barrage had lifted, and they were almost on the beach.

The landing craft grated on sand then, and Martin heard the Navy coxswain yell, "Take 'em away, Lieutenant!"

The steel bulkheads were down, the LCI stopped, and there was nothing between Louie Martin and the beach but his OD shirt.

5

"Hit the beach!" he called and leaped into the shallow waves arching in to the shore. The water was not deep here, but it was cold as ice. Sucking in his breath at the shock, he held his carbine high and pushed strongly through the water. He glanced behind him, saw the platoon pouring out of the boat. "Come on, come on! Move!"

They splashed ashore, moving as fast as possible against the slowing pull of thigh-deep water. A man stumbled and went down.

"Oh, Jesus!" he screamed, in exasperation, staggering up dripping out of the small breakers. It was Pella.

"Clear your piece, Pella," Martin snapped. The jerk probably had the barrel choked with sand.

Now there seemed to be firing all around them. Martin could see flashes and hear gunfire all along the beach, but who the hell was shooting at whom, he couldn't tell. One of the men behind him cut loose at the buildings up ahead. The bullets almost took Martin's head off.

He heard Krueger shout, "Cut that out, goddamnit! No firing—no firing yet!"

"Follow me," Martin shouted. He pounded across the paved street running parallel to the water. He could hear and see other platoons crossing to either side of him. But, strangely, there was no light in any of the buildings he passed. The Eyetie civilians must have been evacuated by the Krauts.

In the dark there was confusion. A little way off to the right, an automatic weapon chattered harshly. A voice screamed, "Cut it out, damnit! We're not Krauts!"

Up from Yellow Beach, Anzio was only a block deep. When Martin passed an imposing stone apartment house he found himself in the clear, under the low bluff that back-stopped the stretched-out town.

"Up on the high ground," he panted to Krueger, whom he heard cursing, rather than saw, in the faint light.

The bluff was sandy and covered with tall cedar trees. Here, in the open, Martin could look out to the sea, where the dark silhouettes of big ships lay three miles off shore. Between the convoy and the beaches passed a steady stream of landing craft, leaving long bright streaks in the black water. There was a lot of light and noise from Red and Green, where the dogfaces of the 3rd had gone ashore, and from the north, a faint sound of firing hung on the early morning wind.

Closer, to his right, the 509th Paratroopers seemed to be shooting up a storm in Nettuno. Martin bit his lip. Could be trouble—but, hell, those hop-heads would shoot at anything. Anybody who'd all join hands and jump out of airplanes . . . . With his running and heavy breathing, his glasses had steamed up. He took them off, blinking against the dark, and rubbed the lenses with an OD handkerchief.

Krueger came up beside him. "I hate to say it, Lieutenant, but it looks like

6

nothin' went wrong." Krueger scratched his long, weathered face unhappily. "For the first time in the history of warfare, nothin' went wrong."

"It will, Sarge," Henry said, moving out of the dark, hot-eyed and nasty-voiced as ever. "You wait. Somebody'll louse this deal up yet."

"No, we made it," Private Pella said, his voice high. "By God, I think this is going to be easy, sir. The Krauts aren't here, or they aren't fighting!"

"Don't *sindig*," the brawny, heavy-set Meyer complained, setting his M-1 butt on the sandy ground.

"What?"

"That's Yiddish for don't count your goddamn chickens too soon," Meyer's rich Gotham accent replied.

"Oh, for Christ's sake, cut out the chatter. You a bunch of recruits?" Krueger said. He dropped into a squat beside Martin. "What now, sir?"

"We wait. Hell, I thought it'd take us two hours to get this far, if we got here at all," Martin said. "We'll have to go back into the town and start clearing it out, but we wait until Battalion gets things straightened out."

"Yeah," Krueger said. He took off his helmet, scratched at his head. "Damn bad fire fight between our own boys could get started down there."

Now another unit moved up on the bluff near them. There were whispered challenges, countersigns. Somebody slapped a rifle butt, laughed.

A captain came along the rows of cedars. "Martin? Where's Martin?"

"Here, sir." Louie stepped out from the trees.

"Good. All your men make it okay? No casualties? Good! Major Dodson says take your boys back along the street, start clearing the port area. The other battalion'll go south, link up with the 509th."

"All right," Martin said. "Let's go."

He led them out of the cedar grove, down the hill and into the main boulevard of Anzio. They clung to the side of the stone edifices, in the shadows.

"Okay, house to house," Martin said. "Don't by-pass anything unless you know damn well it's clear, or someone will get killed. Okay? Krueger, you take that side of the street. Move out."

Caution lay in the young, hard faces as the Rangers heaved up their weapons and moved along the dark street. A large house or villa loomed up before them. "Go in," Martin ordered. He stood back, covering with his carbine as Henry shot the lock off the door.

The villa was dark. Henry swore. "Where the hell's the light switch?" Newton took out his flashlight, swung the light over the room. It was bare except for the dust on the floor. Inside, he felt fairly safe using the light. Besides, it was obvious nobody had disturbed the dust here for some time.

Pella came back from one of the rooms. "Furniture all piled up in there, sir," he reported. "It's all wrapped in burlap, too. Looks like whoever lived here moved out."

7

"Evacuated by the Krauts. That's normal on the coast," Martin said. "Look around good, men. See what's outside."

Meyer came up from the cellar. "Hey, Lieutenant, you know there's nothing but wine cellars down there? Looks like they go on for a mile!"

"Bring any full bottles back?" It was Henry's voice, eager.

"Nah. Only found a couple of empty barrels. The stinkin' Nazis been here first."

Martin grinned. "Come on, we got more to worry about than Dago red."

They went back in the street, pressed on, with a file on each side of the street, in the approved fashion. Men went forward, breaking into buildings while others covered with automatic weapons. Now and then a grenade coughed, a rifle slammed, as the Rangers took no chances. But that was all. No one fired back. There were no Krauts.

"Damnit," Louie Martin told Krueger as they joined at a street junction almost before the port warehouses, "I don't get it. There is supposed to be a Kraut division defending along here."

Krueger gestured with his big left hand. "You know what, Lieutenant? For my money, they're back up in 'the hills, just waitin'.'"

"No. Krauts don't fight that way. Remember Africa, Sicily? The minute you hit a German, the first thing he does is counterattack—hard. Something is fishy here."

Krueger shrugged. "Maybe there just ain't any *Tedeschi*. Maybe they were all sent south, to stop II Corps's offensive at the Rapido River."

Martin said, "There must be forty thousand spies in Naples. We couldn't sail out of there, move a hundred twenty miles up the coast, and still surprise the Germans. Nix, Krueger. I can't buy it."

They pressed on, moving faster now, more carelessly. Waiting for Martin to move out across a small square, Henry asked Pella, "Say, who's this Al Ricovero, the Dago with his name on the walls? Some kind of big shot?"

"That means Air Raid Shelter, you fathead," Pella said disgustedly.

"Yeah? Well, I don't speak the Dago, you know, *no capish*—"

"Shut up," Martin told them, irritably.

Another half-hour, and they met men from the third Ranger battalion that had come ashore at Anzio. None of the three had met any resistance, though they had shot up a few houses here and there. There was still the sound of firing coming down the shoreline, not close, but just enough to keep everyone jumpy. Hell, this was worse than being fired at!

One of Martin's men moved forward. "Sir, Major Dobson's looking for you." He pointed. "Down there by that big palm tree on the avenue."

"Okay."

A knot of Ranger officers gathered, talking quietly in the street. "Hi. You see anything?"

8

"One of my men thinks he got a Kraut."

"How about you, Major Miller?"

"Quiet. The town's clear of enemy—maybe some in the cellars."

Martin recognized Major Alvah Miller, CO of the 3rd Battalion. He stepped up, reported smartly to Major Dobson, his own CO. He didn't see his company commander around. Miller was saying, "Let Colonel Darby know the Navy can come in now, start clearing the port of mines. This is a big break for General Lucas—we can start bringing in supplies pretty quick."

Martin saw other Ranger officers approaching by twos and threes from the dark streets.

"All right," his battalion commander said. "Here's the scoop, men. Apparently we caught the Germans with their pants down. If they have any troops, they are to the north, nearer Rome. But we can count on them bringing up reinforcements quickly—possibly two to four divisions in a couple of days. That's straight from Fifth Army G-2. So the war isn't over yet.

"We're still attached to General Truscott and the 3rd Division. Now that the coast has been cleared, we've got to move inland and establish the beachhead line. We'll have a perimeter around the port about seven miles deep and some fifteen miles long. There's a good highway going north from Anzio toward Albano. Everything east of the road is our country, west side is for the British. Don't cross boundaries. The 3rd Division's right boundary, on the south, is the Mussolini Canal along by the Pontine Marshes."

"Big front," someone said quietly.

"Damn big. But we'll have two more divisions, the 45th and 1st Armored—or at least the best part of 'em—ashore before long. Now, we push out to the beachhead line, give the port a chance to unload a few supplies. I imagine in a day or so we'll blast in toward Cisterna and the Alban Hills, to cut the German roads to the southern front. But first things first. Let's get out to the beachhead line. Watch your steps."

Martin returned to his platoon. "On your feet. It's off to the races again."

The Rangers struck inland, crossing the bluff that towered above the town of Anzio and skirting the thick pine woods that rose up near the sea. The trees grew in thick clumps, with open fields between the stands. The timbered area Seemed to run about five miles. Going through it, Louie Martin thought it would make, a fine supply dump.

Off to his west, in the British zone of advance, the ground looked rough and broken by deep ravines—what the veterans of North Africa called "wadi country." That kind of terrain played the devil with armor, but it was good for infiltration.

To the east and south, in the 3rd Division's zone, the land opened up flatly for miles. The soil itself was marshy, sodden from the rains, but it was crossed by good, paved roads, one to Albano, beyond the Alban Hills, and a

9

highway leading off to Cisterna, a rail center. Beside the main highways there seemed to be a number of flat, paved side roads, too.

Martin studied the terrain keenly in the early dawn. He remembered that this area was supposed to be good for maneuver. But G-2's maps were not too good. They didn't show the gulleys and ravines in the British zone, and didn't indicate that all vehicular traffic would be road-bound elsewhere near Anzio. Martin looked northward, to the high, brooding hill mass called the Colli Laziali, or Alban Hills. From up there, he figured, every inch of the beachhead was visible to Kraut eyes. *We will have to take those hills, and soon,* he thought.

They passed through the wooded area, out into the flat-lands. Here the landscape was dotted with two-storied *poderi,* the plastered-stone Italian farmhouses. This part of Italy was recently reclaimed land, part of Mussolini's big drainage and resettlement project in the Pontine Marshes. The houses were new, modern for Italy, but they were built with the ugly sameness that characterized government projects the world over. In the fields near the houses grazed herds of lean, dark cattle.

Here they encountered their first Italians. While the coast had been cleared by the Germans for security reasons, none of the farmers had been moved from the land. The peasants poured from their stone houses once they realized these passing troops were not *Tedeschi* but *Americani.* The women waved, the men shouted and waved bottles of red wine and forty-octane cognac.

Martin grimly pushed them off. "Keep away from 'em," he ordered. "This isn't liberation day yet!" He grinned, then shouted, "Pella! Knock it off—unless that's your long lost cousin!"

Pella broke off his halting Italian, blushed. "Sir, they say there are *Tedeschi* up ahead—lots of them."

"We'll find 'em," Martin prophesied. "All right, spread out more. Let's go."

They went another mile, and Martin could not see the units on his left. They had apparently pushed ahead of the others. That wasn't good, and he was thinking about holding it up for a bit, when the first automatic fire ripped through the grass. Everybody hit the dirt. Martin cursed as he felt the moisture from the soggy earth soak through his field jacket. *Rrrip! Rrrip!* You didn't have to be a veteran to know that was no American machine gun, he thought sourly.

"That farmhouse—over there!" Sergeant Krueger shouted. *"Tedeschi!"* Krueger, a Dutchman himself, didn't like the word "Kraut."

"Okay," Martin said loudly. "You know what to do. Let's move in!"

He rolled over, cocked his carbine. An officer, he realized, had no business taking part in the fire fight, but you never knew. His own gun might be vital. Everybody to either side of him began firing at the farmhouse. *Pow!*

10

Pow! Pow! Martin saw the stone chips fly from the face of the building. *Whang! Whang!*

Krueger tapped two men, motioned them forward. All three of them ran a few steps to the right, sank down in the marsh grass. They got up, ran again, and now the unmistakable ripping noise of a Schmeisser MP 38 cut through the flat reports of the American rifles. Dirt splattered in front of Krueger, but now he was behind the farmhouse, away from the windows. The squads behind Martin kept up a steady base of fire, pinning the enemy down, keeping them back from the windows.

Krueger crouched beside a window, holding a grenade. He straightened, threw and crouched again. *Blam!* Black smoke spurted out of the windows. Then Krueger and his two men went inside, their submachine guns blazing. Martin got to his feet, motioned the rest of the platoon forward.

As they ran forward, a tall figure in a gray-green overcoat fell from a second-story window. The body turned over in the air, bounced soggily as it hit, the coal-scuttle helmet rolling away on the ground. Behind Martin, Meyer lifted his rifle and fired three times. *Crack!* The prone figure jerked twice, lay still. Martin kept his eyes on the house windows.

Then from the second story Krueger waved. "We got 'em all, Lieutenant."

Meyer was turning the dead German over. Unshaven face, vacant blue eyes, and under the overcoat, the epaulets of a sergeant, with eagle and V-stripe silvery against the green tunic. One of Meyer's bullets had entered his mouth, blowing away the back of his head. Meyer turned away, looking slightly sick.

Krueger came outside, holding up a machine pistol. "Souvenir, Lieutenant?"

"Nuts," Martin, said. "You know better than to pick up stuff. Come on, let's move out."

Just ahead there was a large villa, and men were pouring from it. Martin's men began firing at the villa, and the dark figures scurried back inside. Still firing, Martin's platoon paused at the stone fence.

Pella lofted a grenade through one of the windows. Glass shattered, smoke spurted. Inside someone screamed. Martin shook his head. The Krauts weren't reacting like he expected.

While the rest of the platoon watched and kept up a steady fire on the villa, he ran around the fence, up to the house. Once in a while you had to do it yourself, officer or not, just to show the men you could. He sprayed half a magazine from his carbine into the front door, kicked it down, went inside the front hall.

Bam! Cursing, he leaped back. That was a pistol shot! And a good thing— if the Kraut had used a shoulder weapon he'd be plugged. He pulled the trigger of the carbine twice, watched the German lean over the upstairs railing slowly, then slide over, fall through the air. *What the devil!* Martin thought.

11

Krauts were running around inside in their skivvies. Doors slammed, and voices shouted hoarsely, shrilly.

A young German, no more than nineteen, crossed the main salon, trying to make the back door. Pella, who had now joined Martin, fired three times, the slugs smashing the Nazi against the wall. Another German ran down the corridor under the stairs, screamed as a slug took him in the back. Henry and Meyer were at the windows, firing rapidly into the villa. Bullets were flying everywhere, striking flesh, chipping the walls. *Wkannggg!* A ricochet sang past Martin's left ear, and he ducked. But they were all Ranger bullets.

"Cease fire cease fire!" he bellowed.

As the firing died away, he stepped forward, over the body of the Kraut kid Pella had brought down. He hardly noticed it. It was a rough war, and if you didn't play tough, you were dead.

"Nickt schiessen! Nicht schiessen!" a man was howling from inside an upstairs room. The Germans were coming out now, hands in the air. Martin gaped; there were a hell of a lot of them, more than his platoon.

Krueger, who knew a little *Deutsch*, assembled them outside in the chill morning air, where the rising sun struck dull fire from the bayoneted rifles leveled on the prisoners. Most of the prisoners were in their underwear, shivering.

"Check the villa," Martin ordered. "See if any more are hiding in there." He wheeled, to Krueger. "Find out who's in charge."

"Offizier?" Krueger barked.

All the prisoners shook their heads vigorously. A thin man with gold-rimmed spectacles stepped forward, wincing as Meyer's M-1 swung to cover him. *"Feldwebel,"* the thin man said. In his underclothing, he looked slightly ridiculous, not at all warlike.

Krueger said, "This bird says he's a sergeant."

PFC Henry came out of the villa, grinning, marching two more Germans before him. "What the hell, Lieutenant," he said. "Found these sonsabitches in bed yet!"

Martin said, "Ask the sergeant why they didn't hear the bombardment and shooting."

"They heard it," Krueger answered, after a brief exchange. The Kraut sergeant looked sullen. "He says this was supposed to be a rest camp. These jerks just got here from the Cassino front, all shot up. They just weren't looking for no more war."

"Ask him what outfit they're from."

This time the *Feldwebel* shook his head. "Geneva Conventions," he snapped, and even in German it sounded enough like English so that Martin got it.

Martin said grimly, "We'd better shoot a couple, as an example—"

A German private said something sharply to the *Feldwebel*. The sergeant paled, began to speak rapidly in German. Krueger smiled sourly, said, "Twenty-ninth Panzer Grenadier Division, sir. That's armored infantry—"

"I know. All right, they'll get a rest, for sure—and a nice, long boat ride back to the States." He signaled to Meyer. "You and Henry and Pella, move this bunch back to the beach. That one over there speaks English, I think. Tell him to tell the sergeant to move them out." Martin had seen Kraut POWs before. "Let their own NCO march 'em, it's easier. But watch him. Turn 'em over to the first troops you find back there, and beat it back here."

"We got to take them back?" Meyer asked softly.

"Yes," Martin said, saying something he was soon to remember. "Look, we might get surrounded ourselves sometime. Krueger, what the hell are they hollerin' about now?"

Krueger grinned, spat. "They want to go back for their mess kits."

"Crap. Move 'em out, Meyer."

All in all, about forty Germans were killed that morning, and over two hundred taken prisoner in all parts of the beachhead. It was the same all over—no real resistance. There hadn't been a thousand Germans in the whole area, and none of those had been organized to fight. Six Corps had more men killed and injured landing in the surf from accidents than from enemy fire.

By midmorning, everyone except the British was on the initial beachhead line. The English 1 Division had been held up by mine fields coming in, but an hour later they made contact with the Rangers. The Rangers linked up with the paratroops from Nettuno, and General Truscott sent a patrol from the 3rd Division to meet the jump-boys. Everything was copasetic.

"Duck soup," said PFC Pella, coming back from the beach to find Martin's platoon digging in. "There goes your Battle of Anzio, sir." He was grinning. He had stopped to have coffee with some Italians, and he had liberated two bottles of Alberti gin, now bulging comfortably under his jacket.

"Crap," Martin said, absently. He turned his thin face back toward the blue gleam of the Tyrrhenian Sea to the west. It wasn't very far to the beaches, and from there he could hear the scream of plane engines, the *crump-crump* of bursting bombs. The *Luftwaffe* was up, anyway. A couple of columns of black smoke spiraled lazily upward in the still air.

He pushed his steel-rimmed GI glasses back up on his nose, thinking, if he had any sense, he'd be in the Quartermaster, with his eyes. But that was a lot of crap, too. He had to be in the front of it, wherever it was, and he'd as soon be a eunuch as be in uniform and in a noncombat job. In fact, if it wasn't for his damn eyes, he'd . . . "Crap, Pella," he repeated. "This damn fight is just beginning."

2

Operation Shingle

"They will put me ashore with inadequate forces and get me in a serious jam. Then, who will take the blame?"—From the diary of Major General John P. Lucas, CG, VI U.S. Corps.

Four months before Louis Martin and his platoon of Rangers stormed ashore at Anzio, the American and British forces in the Mediterranean had landed at Salerno. After a short, desperate battle, during which they were almost thrown back into the sea, the Allied foothold had been firmly established.

The slow march up the Italian boot began, every inch of the way against stubborn German resistance. The Allies expected a quick entry into Rome, for they felt the Germans would do the logical thing, which was to retreat to the mountain ranges north of the Eternal City. Such a move would shorten German lines and yet deny the Allies the greater part of the Italian industrial machine, which was located in the north.

But this was not to be.

Reichsführer Adolf Hitler, acting as commander-in-chief of the German armed forces, squirmed in an agony of indecision in the fall of 1943. In Italy he had two senior, seasoned commanders: Kesselring and Rommel. But they

14

held opposing views as to what German strategy should be, and for almost two months after the September landings at Salerno, neither was placed in sole command in Italy, nor was German policy decided.

Finally, in early November, 1943, Hitler called a fateful conference in Berlin. He would listen to both Rommel and Kesselring, and he would have two separate drafts of orders on his desk as he listened. From this meeting would come one of the most important German command decisions of the war.

As the conference opened, *General feldmarschall* Erwin Rommel was pained. He had told the *Führer* his position, and he had backed it with facts, not the dream stuff the General Staff was beginning to wallow in. And now—when Erwin Rommel was agitated, he always reverted to his native broad Swabian—all he could do was sit here like a *stolten* bottle with a mouth full of teeth and one finger up his behind, while the *Führer* chewed his facts to bits and spat them out like pieces of carpet.

"I am sick of generals who want to retreat! You do not win wars by retreating, *Herr Feldmarschall!*"

"That is not the point, *mein Führer,*" Rommel said, flushing. "We cannot throw the Allies out of Italy. No matter. Italy cannot decide the war; the Alps are always between us and the south. The thing to do is to pull back north of Rome, fortify the Apennines. Thus we shorten our lines, while the *Allierte* extend theirs. Otherwise, we hold ground, but tie down too many of our divisions."

Erwin Rommel did not say it aloud, but he was thinking what most of the ranking commanders of the *Wehrmacht* were thinking that November of 1943. The Reich's strategic reserve had gone down the drain at Stalingrad and Cape Bon, in Africa. With those troops, Hitler's grand concept of *Festung Europa*—Fortress Europe—could have been a reality.

Now, Rommel didn't know where the OKW—the *Oberkommando der Wehrmacht,* the High Command—was going to get the troops to hurl back the projected Allied invasion. It was going to be touch and go in the spring of '44, even without thirty to forty German divisions tied down in the mud of southern Italy. But the same architect of Stalingrad and Tunisia was still at the drawing board.

"Pull back—pull back!" Hitler snapped. "That is all I hear from my generals now. A fine lot. I could replace all of you with corporals from the line—*they* would know what to do!"

Rommel swallowed, said nothing.

"What you do not realize," the *Führer* continued, "is the strategic value of Rome itself. It is Mussolini's capital—it would be a great coup for Churchill and Roosevelt to capture it. Think of the effect on the enemy populations! And on the neutrals—what of Turkey?"

15

"And of the Balkans, *mein Führer,*" *General feldmarschall* Kesselring put in suddenly. "With southern Italy firmly in our grasp, the Allies could strike to the Balkans, cut off our troops, meet the Russians—"

"*Natürlich.* The Allies would be great fools if they did not think of the Balkans," Hitler said triumphantly. He picked up a pencil, began to tap it nervously.

Rommel looked at Kesselring sourly. "Smiling Albert"was senior to him; he had been a field marshal when Rommel had still worn only a junior *generalleutnant's* epaulets. But Erwin Rommel knew he was the Reich's premier fighting general, and he had both the Oak Leaves to his Knight's Cross and his field marshal's baton from the *Führer's* hand for his work with the Afrika Corps. And there was the rub—what the *Führer had bestowed, the Führer* could take away. Erwin Rommel cleared his throat, fell silent.

Kesselring's bluff, handsome face lit up as he poured on the charm. "*Mein Führer,* with no disrespect to Rommel here, we can hold the *Allierte* easily south of Rome. All winter, at the least. The Todt Organization can make the southern mountains impregnable. I personally have been over the terrain. Before the war, the Italian Royal War College used this area to illustrate grund perfect for defense."

Trust Smiling Albert to bring in the Eyeties, Rommel thought morosely. Kesselring had always been an Italophile, spoke the language, loved them. He had entirely too high an opinion of their abilities, including the value of Old Muss to the Reich. But Axis partner or not, Rommel knew the Eyeties couldn't pull their weight. Already their provisional government had booted Musso out, made peace with the Allies. The only reason *Il Duce* ruled in North Italy was the fact that Rommel's Fourteenth Army held the country firmly in control, keeping the Fascisti in office.

Hitler brushed his dark forelock back from his eyes, fingered his stiff mustache. His dark eyes brooded, gleaming. *Now we get another decision,* Rommel guessed. *Herr Gott, let it be a right one! Let us pull back in Italy, save some divisions to oppose the Allies when they come storming across the English Channel!*

But Adolf Hitler shot Erwin Rommel a glance that showed plainly he had never forgiven the *Wüstenfuchs* his unordered, retreat at El Alamein. Of course, Hitler had finally agreed to that, on the record, and he had sent the major who transmitted his personal order to stand and die to the labor battalions as a scapegoat, claiming the whole thing was an error.

But Hitler's heart had not changed. His eyes said plainly that he wished Rommel *had stood* and died on the African sands, even if such loss would have been to no avail. Any other course smacked to the *Führer* of personal betrayal. Under those eyes, Rommel was glad for the first time that he was one of the Reich's greatest heroes. Even Hitler did not place the Oak Leaves on a man one day, then order him shot the next.

16

"One of you is talking sense," Hitler said succinctly, in his high voice. "I am pleased I still have *some* loyal servants left."

Rommel looked studiously at the tapestried walls, avoiding both Hitler's and Smiling Albert's eyes. Rome, indeed! Rome was only important to the Pope—and then only as a symbol, he brooded. His tanned, blunt face, with its thrusting chin and straight nose, grew grim.

In this day, cities, symbols, meant nothing in war. Wars were won by movement, encirclement, the smashing of whole armies in the field. Cities, even capitals, meant very little to the outcome. The *Wehrmacht* must not be spread thin, trying to hold every useless centimeter of ground—*ach*, that was how the French and British had lost in '40, trying to protect places, sacred French soil, while whole armies went down the armored German maw. Hitler could not be so stupid—to tie down divisions now was the same as to lose them. *Ja*, you tied down the enemy, too, and bled him—but Germany was herself turning pale from that game!

But smiling, Hitler lifted the two drafts that lay on his desk. He had had two made because he could not make up his mind: Rommel's plan or Kesselring's. Now he threw one draft in the waste hopper, signed the remaining one with a flourish.

"*Herr Feldmarschall,*" he said to Kesselring, "you are appointed Commanding General, Army Group 'C'—and Commander in Chief, Southwest."

Kesselring's plan had won. Kesselring had told Hitler what he wanted to hear. Not one meter of holy ground held by German arms would be surrendered—but German blood would flow lavishly in the rocky Italian soil.

Smiling Albert has one genius, Rommel thought to himself. *Probably no leader in all history knows better how, to lose a war slowly.* The Americans and British would pay and pay, but in the end it would all come to nothing, unless the force was found to smash the cross-Channel invasion.

"Rommel, you are excused. We shall find something for you to do in France."

Erwin Rommel left the Presence. He was understanding more and more the guarded remarks, the half-said sentences, that some of his colleagues among the generals were using. He himself was too loyal to say those things, even think them—yet. But he was being shaken, little by little.

First, there had been the *Führer's* order to execute all captured British Commandos. That order he had ignored. Africa had been far from Berlin, and he could get away with it. Then had come the fiasco at El Alamein, when Hitler had ordered him to lose his beloved Korps. Later, Hitler had made certain all the Afrika Korps was destroyed at Cape Bon, when by swallowing a little pride, retreating in time, it could have been saved. And now this decision to fight for Italy meter by meter.

Going out into the cold November air, looking at the bleak, damaged

17

expanse of Berlin, Rommel suddenly felt an enormous nostalgia for the old days, for the Desert. Back in the desert there had been no hostile civilians underfoot, no political officers, no SS, no—Corporal Hitler.

He shivered and wondered how it was all going to end.

Adolf Hitler had made his decision. German divisions, German engineers poured into Italy throughout the long month of November, 1943. The Allied advance began to slow. By December it had ground to a dead halt. And a few days before Christmas, Major General John P. Lucas, commanding the VI U.S. Army Corps, sat in his command post south of a river called the Rapido, watching the rain pour down.

Outside the stone building that housed the VI Corps staff the world was a sea of mountains and mud. It was always raining, Johnny Lucas groaned inwardly, and if the cold and dampness got to a corps commander, it must be pure hell for the poor bastards up there in the foxholes and unheated stone farm huts.

Johnny Lucas moved stiffly to the door and looked out into the sleeting rain, watching a file of helmeted, ponchoed, bearded men slog by miserably in the mud. He sighed. Johnny Lucas was almost fifty-four years old—his birthday was January 14, 1944, less than three weeks away—and he felt every year of it.

Artillery boomed hollowly in the misty, rain-shrouded mountains. *Brroom-brroom.* The lines were not moving now, but every minute of each day and night somebody was killed. It was almost as bad to stop and slug it out as it was to move forward in the attack.

After Salerno, when the American Fifth Army got a firm foothold on the Italian boot, all they talked about back in the States and up at Fifteenth Army Group HQ—that Limey-run boars' nest—was Rome, Rome, Rome. The high, high brass had figured the Germans would pull back in Italy; Rome would be taken easily; and there would be a nice, fat victory to show the home folks. Of course, there had been victories on the Allied side, Stalingrad and Tunisia. Those two campaigns had broken the back of the Axis, destroyed armies Hitler could never replace. But the home folks, and the politicians, did not think in terms of armies destroyed, strategic reserves broken. They thought in terms of cities, capitals, glowing symbols they could see on their home-front maps. Rome, the Eternal City, Mussolini's capital, was the greatest symbol of them all.

But it hadn't gone that way. The Huns had poured division after division into Italy. The famous Todt Engineers worked day and night forging the Winter Line. G-2 didn't have to tell Johnny Lucas that both the German divisions and the Todt Organization were first-rate; he had seen the broken bodies carried back from the 34th and 3rd Division fronts. And to Johnny Lucas, no symbol in the world was worth one dead GI.

Lucas left the doorway, went back to the big corps operations map. He took off his steel spectacles, ran a thin hand through his frazzled white hair. Because of that hair, those glasses and his long nose and pointed chin, his staff called him "Foxy Grandpa"behind his back. Johnny Lucas didn't mind; he knew everyone in Italy, both the generals and the small fry, was fond of him. Johnny Lucas was that kind of man.

Looking at the operations map, with its blue and red symbols, Lucas did not see hills, regiments, corps and divisions. He kept seeing dogfaces lying dead in the mud; he kept seeing the tired, bearded faces with vacant eyes, the faces of infantrymen pushed to the very limit of human endurance. Because that was the kind of war this was.

There were the mountains, rocky, forbidding, bare, towering over rapid little streams and narrow, misty valleys. You had to go up the narrow valleys—and the Huns were on the mountains. So first the artillery, of which, thank God, there was plenty, plastered the mountains. Then, reluctantly, for they didn't like close support missions in rough ground, the Twelfth Air Force flew a few sorties to blast the German lines. After that, there was nothing to do but send the dogfaces forward—for neither the Air Force nor the artillery could take ground.

Then it was the Hun's turn. First, his artillery, tearing the assembly areas, sending the wounded streaming back. Then, when in spite of shot and shell the Americans came on, he came up out of his nice, snug bunkers and fortified holes, set his MG 42s on their tripods, zeroed in his Screaming Meemies. *Brrrp-blam! Amerikäner kaput!* But stumbling, bleeding, falling, dying for each inch of the way, the dogfaces finally went over the hill, shooting, grenading, bayoneting.

When they reached the crest—*wham!*—here came the Hun counterattack, guns blazing, each soldier eager for the Iron Cross. And when that was finally beaten off, and more lay dead in the ice-rimed mud, and the dead-tired company commanders reported their positions secured, the generals could go up front and peer through the fog with their field glasses.

And they saw another hill, just like the one they had taken, and beyond it a hundred more. That was the kind of war this was.

Lucas went to the door again, watching a train of pack mules slog past, going back down the mountain. Some of the mules bore dirty, stiffened bodies. Bodies like poor Kirtley's, killed on the south spur of Mount Lungo, like poor—their names were legion, Lucas thought. We have made eight miles, and lost two thousand men the mile.

Who the hell wanted Rome anyway?

He knew the answer to that. Winston Churchill passionately desired Rome, and that meant all the British generals wanted Rome, too. Even President Roosevelt had put his oar in, needling Mark Clark, the Fifth Army Commander. "Keep driving it all you've got," he'd told Clark, "and Rome will be ours, and more beyond."

Johnny Lucas knew the war wasn't going to be won in Italy. That would come when Eisenhower's forces smashed across the Channel next spring. He could understand why the British made such a big deal out of Italy, of course. The Mediterranean had always been important to them, life line to India and all that. But if they kept insisting on Rome, and influencing the American High Command, a hell of a lot of people were going to die—and for what Lucas felt was nothing.

Johnny Lucas had been a fine corps commander. He was well thought of by the Chief of Staff, General Marshall, and he had served as Eisenhower's deputy. He had replaced General Omar Bradley as corps commander. He had given it all he had.

A long time later, he would realize he had given it too much. The bloody fighting, the endless lack of success, had left him tired and dispirited. Johnny Lucas, still well thought of in the higher echelons of command, had seen one broken body too many in the mountains of southern Italy.

Johnny Lucas, watching the rain, did not know the high brass were talking back in North Africa, at Tunis, or that within a month they would put him ashore at Anzio with his VI Corps and attached troops. For in Tunis plans were being made to end the stalemate, and in these plans Major General Lucas figured prominently.

The one thing the high brass did not know about Johnny Lucas, general, gentleman and soldier, was what was in his heart and mind. This they would discover much too late.

On Christmas Day, 1943, the HQ offices finally decided the plan that would send Louie Martin and his platoon running up the beaches at Anzio. It had taken time, and it would take more time, to iron out the details. It takes a lot of time to make arrangements to send fifty thousand men into desperate combat.

Tunis was a rotten spot to spend Christmas Day—but it could have been a lot worse, Brian Rainey kept telling himself. No, Tunis wasn't so bad, especially if you were a full lieutenant at last—he looked sidewise at his shoulder loops again, seeing the heavy black second pip pinned comfortably there—and a junior officer on Army Group staff. Sir Harold Alexander wasn't hard to get along with, though when you were as junior as Brian Rainey, you rarely came into close contact with the Commanding General.

But the best thing of all, outside of being warm, clean, out of danger and well fed, was that one actually knew what the bloody hell was going on in the war. It was good to visit Montgomery's HQ, or the HQ of that American, Clark, over there in Italy. All the subalterns, and quite a lot of the colonels, too, asked you what was going on.

Take this conference in the next room, now—something was in the wind. Prime Minister Churchill had flown out from England just to confer with Sir Harold and that Yank general who was commanding the theater, Eisenhower. Brian smiled, touched his sandy mustache. With a name like that, the bloke ought really to be on the other side, eh?

And while they were having a fine dinner, all the trimmings, the staff was kept out here on their bottoms waiting for the show to pop. Not that they had any kick. They had gotten a few bottles of the Old Man's bubbly, and even a handful of really decent cigars. That was one thing about the PM— wherever he went, he had the best. And good for him, Brian Rainey thought.

After a bit, one of Sir Harold's American aides came out of the main dining room. Grimsley, a captain who'd been aide to General Truscott of the 3rd Division, and a good man.

"Scratch HERCULES and PIGSTICK—enter SHINGLE," the Yank said.

"SHINGLE—the Anzio go?" Brigadier Kenneth Strong's nose twitched. As theater G-2, he was always on the spot. Sometimes it seemed the top red-hats expected him to have a teletypewriter straight into Berlin, with the Huns handing him a copy of each of their messages. "They're back to putting the Yank 3rd Division ashore below Rome?"

"No, the Prime Minister's agreed to at least two divisions—one American, one British. Complicates supply and command, but they all feel it should be a joint Allied effort. The PM said it will astonish the world, and certainly frighten Kesselring, to land behind the German lines."

Strong laughed. "Aye, we may astonish the world—but *Herr Kesselring* doesn't frighten easily."

Brigadier Teren Airey, the intelligence officer from Sir Harold Alexander's Fifteenth Army Group staff, smiled. He was a much blander individual than Strong. "You are thinking like the Nazis now, Strong."

"In my job, I have to," Strong replied moodily.

"Mr. Rainey, will you help me set up some of these maps in here?" Sir Harold Alexander's British aide called through the door. Brian leaped to his feet and entered the exalted atmosphere.

Around the table he recognized his own commander, Sir Harold, slender, neat and trim as always, his pencil mustache carefully waxed. Next to him sat Yank Theater Commander "Ike"Eisenhower, his sparsely-haired head shining pink in the electric lamp glow. Eisenhower looked glum. Across the table sat Sir Henry Maitland Wilson, who was soon to replace Eisenhower, for the Med was now to be a British show all around; Eisenhower had already been ordered to England to command the projected cross- Channel attack. One look at Sir Henry told one why he was known as "Jumbo."

And there was Churchill, the old fighter himself, eyes glaring, cheeks pink, voice dripping wrath and glorious phrases straight out of the King James Version. Amid all the stars and brass, it was plain to see who really commanded here. Churchill was at his best when it was rough going, and the PM was determined to change the stalemate in the Med.

"The only way a decision will be forced in Italy is by an amphibious landing near Rome. General Alexander agrees with me. General Wilson is new, has no command, and must perforce be an observer. What is your opinion, Ike?"

Eisenhower shrugged. "I won't be here when SHINGLE is carried out. I think that makes me an observer, too, in a way. However, I am not optimistic, sir. I think the Germans will fight, not withdraw, as Sir Harold proposes they will do. We don't have the sort of numerical superiority to assure success."

"We've got to do something," Churchill growled. "The Germans are making us look bad with their stubborn defense. We have got to take Rome, and soon."

Eisenhower shrugged, smiled. "Well, I've given my advice."

"Then, it is decided, gentlemen," Churchill said brusquely. "Alexander and I are in substantial agreement. We shall gather the naval forces to put two divisions ashore below Rome, with other divisions to follow. With the landings, Montgomery's Eighth Army will demonstrate on the Italian eastern front, while Clark's Fifth, with II Corps, will attack across the Rapido in front of Cassino. The pressure on the Nazis will be enormous. With their flank threatened, the southern front must pull back. We must accept the obvious, thinking of the prize to be gained."

Well, thought Brian Rainey, that was it—the PM had cast the die.

"Now," Churchill growled, lighting up a fresh 71/4-inch English Market Selection Havana, "we'll hear the seamy side of the question. Get the intelligence chaps in."

Even Rainey knew this was not exactly the way a military decision was made—but then, he understood, matter of high policy, political matters, entered into this also. He finished tacking up the map, stood unobtrusively to one side.

Now it was Brigadier Strong's show, as Allied Forces HQ G-2. "Sir," Strong said in his pessimistic voice, "I confess to being skeptical of SHINGLE. Adolf Hitler is well aware of the political importance of Rome. He has no desire to lose it just now."

"All right—what are the Nazis likely to do then?"

"Fight. Fight like the devil, sir. And they've got the stuff to do it with." Strong's cultured voice droned on. "A division in Yugoslavia—the 715th Infantry Division in the south of France—doing nothing at present. And von Mackensen's Fourteenth German Army, in North Italy, uncommitted. I submit, sir, these divisions can be moved, and quickly. The enemy is too strong."

The generals around the table looked at each other. But it was obvious the Prime Minister had not changed his mind. After all, he had made it up before listening to the G-2. Politely, General Alexander said, "Thank you, Brigadier." Strong withdrew.

"My own staff doesn't quite agree with that," Alexander told the group. "I have an estimate drawn up by Terence Airey, my G-2. He's in charge of intelligence in northern Italy, and he feels it is highly unlikely that the Hun will move any troops from the north. And it follows that any major attempt to seal off our beachhead at Anzio will fatally weaken the German Cassino front. In fact, the very possibility of having their communications cut behind the XIV German Corps—von Senger's command—may force them to withdraw. I might say, most everyone on my staff agrees," Sir Harold added, smiling.

Lieutenant Brian Rainey hid the smile that almost came to his lips. Terence Airey knew damned well the nabobs wanted the SHINGLE show, and if one were good, one could make an intelligence estimate show anything. And after all, the Hun *was* whipped. There was simply no point in the buggers throwing more troops down the drain in Italy. When one looked at the big, strategic maps, it was plain to see that the Axis was ringed, defeated. All that remained was to make the bastards realize it.

"Very good," Sir Harold said, his keen face affable but determined. "I shall inform General Clark to make the VI Corps ready for the operation toward the end of January." All the brass rose, stood chatting.

Taking down the maps, Lieutenant Brian Rainey thought, *A damn good show. Catch the dirty beggars with their pants down, snatch Rome in a matter of days.* All the same he decided, he was rather glad he wouldn't be in on it. The proper place to fight a war was on the staff.

The decision made at Tunis on Christmas Day reached Lieutenant General Mark W. Clark's Fifth Army HQ on December 28, 1943. Clark's Fifth Army Would provide the forces for SHINGLE, and it could hardly be said pure joy reigned in that particular part of Italy.

Colonel Howard, Fifth Army G-2, was raising hell.

He told General Clark, "I understand all this. Of course the Gustav Line is going to be a tough nut to crack, and an end run up to Anzio to hit the Krauts in the ass end makes sense. But I don't agree with this estimate by 15th Group Intelligence. Landing at Anzio is not going to maneuver the Krauts out of their sweet setup along the Rapido and at Cassino!"

Mark Clark looked at his G-2 unhappily over his long nose. He told Howard that General Alexander had not asked whether or not Fifth Army liked the plan. It had been presented to Clark as an irrevocable decision made on high levels. They were stuck with it. He said, "Besides, I rather like the idea; it has possibilities. I told Alexander that."

"The enemy will probably fight a tough delaying action in the south, and he will definitely send more forces to seal off the beachhead. The thing is very risky," Howard said again, making his point. "Now my experience has been that British intelligence is excellent—better than ours; they've been at it longer. But they don't always state their true opinions. They like to jolly the troops, damnit! I think Fifteenth Army Group's estimate was made deliberately optimistic to fit the decision already made at Tunis."

Howard's objections impressed Mark Clark deeply. After all, he had selected Johnny Lucas to head the corps landing at Anzio, and Lucas was a good friend. Clark didn't want to get Lucas in trouble if it could be prevented. He mentioned to Howard that the Air Force felt it could isolate the battlefield, prevent German reinforcements from arriving.

"I submit, sir," replied Howard, "that so far they haven't been able to do more than make glowing estimates of what they are going to be able to do—someday. Air can't strangle the battlefield in this kind of mountainous terrain, in the bad winter flying weather particularly."

At the end of the discussion, Clark told Howard to write up his own estimate and present it to him.

Howard went back to his desk and began to write: "An attack on the coast in the vicinity of Anzio by a force the size of a corps will become an emergency to be met by all the resources and strength available to the German High Command in Italy. . . ."

General Lucas now received the word that on or about January 20, 1944 his VI Corps would make an amphibious landing near Anzio. This was less than three weeks away—and when this word arrived, the atmosphere at VI Corps HQ made that of Fifth Army seem jubilant by comparison.

Lucas called Clark and demanded that his corps be taken out of line at once to prepare for the operation. Clark agreed to VI Corps's relief on January 3, 1944. Lucas wanted more time, but he was told the date for the landings had already been set—January 20—because after that date most of the landing craft in the Mediterranean Theater were to be sent to England, to marshal for the coming cross-Channel invasion. Lucas was ordered to send his G-3, Colonel William H. Hill, and his G-4, Colonel E. J. O'Neill, to Marrakech, Morocco, where Churchill was resting, to meet with Allied Force HQ to map out final details as to troops and shipping.

And he was told that General Alexander had called a high-powered conference of all major staffs involved for January 9, to iron out the last-minute wrinkles.

On that date Lucas met with Generals Alexander and Clark. Fifteenth

Army Group staff and the staffs of Fifth Army and VI Corps were in attendance, sitting nervously, each officer waiting for his chance to perform, each officer taking copious notes. Lucas, entering, saw the hushed atmosphere, and he realized that SHINGLE had become the most important operation, at least temporarily, in the war.

Alexander was getting up, after the civilities had been passed. "Gentlemen, at Marrakech Operation SHINGLE has been scheduled to take place on January 22, with Major General Lucas' VI Corps. General Lucas will have General Penney's Division and General Truscott's American 3rd for the initial assault, with attached units, such as Commandos and Rangers. Later, elements of the U.S. 45th and 1st Armored will be landed, with complete corps and Army supporting forces. There is no point in further discussion of these points."

Alexander looked around carefully. He was an erect, slim officer, brilliant but not assuming. He had the drive of a Montgomery or Patton, Lucas thought, but without the flamboyance. Lucas realized Alexander was one of the best Allied commanders, although personally, he had never cared for the British. Too arrogant, too cold . . .

What was Sir Harold saying? "Mr. Churchill has said this operation will startle the world, and it will certainly frighten Kesselring."

Maybe, Lucas thought. *I haven't seen many frightened Krauts lately. Kesselring seems to be a tough cookie.* Damnit, he just didn't have any confidence in the British. Look at the faces over there, where the 15th Group staff sat—nonchalant, nothing like the looks on the faces of his own colonels. *Damnit. I am a lamb being led to slaughter. I should be entitled to at least one bleat.*

Lucas stood up. He looked at Mark Clark's long, lean, schoolmasterish form. Clark was looking serious, as usual. Maybe it wouldn't do any good, but he'd have his say, anyway. God, he felt tired. . . .

"General, the target date is too soon. It gives me no time for rehearsal. This is a terribly complicated maneuver, putting a whole corps ashore behind enemy lines. I need more training time. In the 3rd Division, the turnover of infantry lieutenants has been 115 percent. The men that knew the answers are gone."

"We have discussed that, General. Mr. Churchill is aware that most of the men with the British 1st and U.S. 3rd Divisions who have taken part in landings are gone. But even one NCO per squad or platoon who is experienced is enough."

Lucas shrugged and sat down. He knew he would be overruled anyway. But he thought. *All the reasons being advanced for this speed are phony. The real reasons cannot be military. They want to get Rome before the cross-Channel invasion begins, that must be it. . . .*

Alexander continued, "It is quite possible that this operation will turn into

25

a major disaster for the Germans. Its success may even make the projected cross-Channel invasion of Europe unnecessary."

No doubt you'd all like that, Lucas thought bleakly. None of the British seemed to have much joy in the idea of mucking around in Hitler's heartland—at least not till the Russians had had at the Krauts a little more. But diddling around down here in the Mediterranean for limited objectives—this was a hell of a way to kill people.

The conference was breaking up. Sir Harold Alexander came over to Lucas, told him, "We have every confidence in you. That is why you were picked." *I wish I could say the same,* Lucas thought to himself.

And here was Sir Andrew Cunningham, Allied Naval Commander in the Med., saying bluffly, "The chances are seventy to thirty that, by the time you reach Anzio, the Germans will be north of Rome."

Johnny Lucas smiled slightly behind his steel-rimmed glasses, his pale eyes tired. "Apparently everybody but me is in on the German intentions." He told himself, almost desperately, that these higher commanders must have intelligence information not available down at VI Corps.

Johnny Lucas had so far seen no fleeing Germans. Quite the opposite. Sure, the Kraut generals might know they had already lost the war—but they had not so far let the information seep down to the lower echelons. On the ground they were still fighting like hell. If they put him on an isolated beachhead with outnumbered forces, with barely adequate supply transport by sea, he was going, to be in trouble.

He went back to his HQ, and later that night he wrote in his diary: "Army has gone nuts again. The general idea seems to be that the Germans are licked and fleeing in disorder and nothing remains but to mop up. . . . *I haven't seen the desperate fighting I have during the past four months without learning something.*"

At VI Corps the maps were unrolled, and the pointers went to a place called Anzio.

It lay thirty miles south of Rome, a little coastal resort town. It contained beaches suitable for landings. The area around it was open, and seemed good for maneuver. Finally, the area had good roads leading up to the Alban Hills—Colli Laziali—twenty miles inland.

They were only fifteen miles south of Rome, and through them passed both Highways 6 and 7, the main enemy routes of communication to the southern front. All roads still led to Rome, and whoever held the Colli Laziali had those roads. Furthermore, the hill mass was the last barrier from which Rome might be defended by the Germans.

"Land at Anzio, cut across to the Colli Laziali," Alexander had instructed. "The main enemy communications are cut, and the rear of the German XIV Corps at Cassino is threatened. At the very least, the Hun will have to weaken the southern front to meet the landings in his rear, thus opening an avenue to Rome."

Tactically, the plan was sound. An assault landing in conjunction with a strong push by Clark's Fifth Army in the south, the two to link up. Tactically sound—if the enemy did what they were expected to do.

Sir Harold's Operation Instruction 32, dated January 2, 1944, came down to Mark Clark's HQ. It read: "The object of the Anzio operation is to cut the enemy's main communication in the Colli Laziali southeast of Rome, and to threaten the rear of the German XIV Corps."

But at Mark Clark's HQ Colonel Howard and his boys were still raising hell about the deal. Clark, as an American general, was not completely subservient to Alexander, as Sir Harold well knew. Clark was not disposed to tie Johnny Lucas' hands, make him push inland too fast and possibly lose his whole corps. If VI Corps was lost, Clark would also be ruined. So, listening to his staff, Clark translated Sir Harold's English into American as follows, in Fifth Army Field Order 5, January 12, 1944: "*Mission:* Fifth Army will launch attacks in the Anzio area—(a) to seize and secure a beachhead in the vicinity of Anzio; (b) *advance on the Colli Laziali.*"

Then he sent Brigadier General Don W. Brann, his G-3, down to Lucas to explain the order. Whether Lucas was to advance to or merely *toward* the Alban Hills was going to be up to Lucas, as he saw fit. On the beaches of Anzio, Johnny Lucas was going to have to make one of the most agonizing command decisions of this or any war.

After the plans had been firmed and the orders cut, the remaining days before the operation had passed swiftly. As always before such an attack, there was too much to do, too little time in which to do it.

Fifth Army had ordered the 36th Division to attack on the southern front, near Cassino, to support the landings. And the Tommies of the British 1 Division and the soldiers of the American 3rd had rolled down to Naples. There, in the blue harbor, the LSTs and LCTs had waited. Singing or grousing, as became their nature, they had gone aboard. They had ribbed the bloody Navy, and the bloody Navy had passed it back.

Then there had been the interminable briefings. The men who would do the fighting had learned where they were going, After the briefings, some of the men had written long letters home. In the officers' quarters the midnight oil had burned late.

In his diary, General Lucas had written, before he gave the order that sent Louie Martin and his platoon storming ashore: "I must keep from thinking of the fact that my order will send these men into a desperate attack."

General Lucas was still not sold on the Anzio operation. In this frame of mind, he had ordered fifty thousand ashore at Anzio, into an action which was to turn into a desperate gamble and a fight for survival.

3

"The Führer Demands..."

"If I am to be accused of something, thank God I am accused of attacking instead of retreating."—Mark W. Clark, writing of the Rapido failures

"The heroic sacrifices of the 36th Division undoubtedly drew the Germans away from our landings at Anzio."—Robert P. Patterson, Secretary of War.

Down at Naples, General Lucas' VI Corps had embarked. Soon the convoy would be steaming straight out to sea, heading west at first to confuse any German spies who might be watching, then swinging back north after darkness had fallen. In just a few hours the LCIs would be lowered, and the naval rocket ships would plaster the beaches with flame and steel at Anzio, and the Rangers would splash through the surf.

But in war, when an attack is planned on one front, good tactical planning also calls for a diversion. It is good to hit the enemy; it is better to hit him in two places instead of one. And it is best of all to suck his forces away from the place you intend to hit him, if you can.

Along the stalemated southern front, below Cassino, the 36th Infantry Division had been signally honored by being selected for one of the dirtiest jobs of World War II. A day before the Anzio landings, they would try to smash across the Rapido River, engage the German forces, and force the Germans to send all their reserves in the Anzio area southward. Eventually, they were to break through the German defenses and link up with the Anzio beachhead. Or that was the way the orders read. . . .

So it was that Captain William P. Condett, Heavy Weapons Company Commander, 3rd Battalion, 141st Infantry, 36th Division, shivered in his dirty field jacket in the assembly area, waiting for the attack across the Rapido to begin. Goddamn, the fog was cold! And everything seemed to have gone to hell already, even before 3rd Battalion could move out.

Willie Condett pushed back his steel helmet, ran stubby fingers through his short, sandy hair. Under his heavy brows, his pale blue eyes were troubled. "Damn!" he said aloud, in his soft San Antonio drawl. "This operation's fouled up worse'n the San Antonio Transit System—"

Before the war, Willie Condett had driven a bus back home.

Willie Condett was all soldier. He had joined the Texas National Guard back in high school, and in 1940, when he was twenty-eight, he had finally won his gold bars. He had come overseas with Texas' own 36th Division, and he had been in the front of it ever since.

Willie was thinking that this assembly area was a hell of a place to spend the night. For the Kraut artillery had found the range and was throwing shells in freely. Hell, the whole area, from the Rapido River two miles back, was under shell fire!

All afternoon fourteen battalions of artillery had blazed away, till the hillsides themselves seemed afire. A shell had been fired for each six square yards over there, and Tac Air had made a few runs, too. And with dark, 1st Battalion had moved out to lead the assault across the Rapido. Third Battalion should have moved out, too, long ago. But midnight had passed, and now, in the early hours of January 21, 1944, while the Anzio convoy was at sea, 3rd Battalion still shivered in its assembly area, awaiting word to move.

The rifle battalions of Willie's 141st Infantry Regiment were to attack across the Rapido just north of Sant' Angelo after dark, while south of them their sister battalions from the 143rd would cross the Gari River and drive up the Liri Valley. It seemed a good plan; the two regiments would link up and continue the drive on Rome. In addition, an attack now, on the twenty-first, would give the poor jokers who were going on that end run up to Anzio a break.

But the Rapido Valley was a wide, flat plain ringed with high peaks, from which the Germans had excellent observation. Also, they had recently held all this terrain, and they had been liberal with their damned AP and

Teller mines. Even worse, the bastards had diverted waters from the river to make the ground marshy and impossible to American armor. There was no cover in the Rapido Valley, and the German artillery had had plenty of time to register in.

Without armor-protected firepower to assist in the assault, it was going to be OD shifts and raw nerve against German fire and steel.

And there was another thing that bothered Willie Condett. The division G-2 had estimated the enemy over there had dug in nine battalions. The Infantry School still taught that you had to have numerical superiority to take the offensive, and right now they didn't have it. Willie shivered again, cursing the cold numbly.

The rumor was that General Walker, the 36th Division's commander, had twice asked clarification of his orders to attack—especially the siting of the proposed river crossings. The "S"Bend, right in the bare-ass middle of the front, had been picked by II Corps, and somebody was off their rocker. The river was only forty-five feet wide there, but it was twelve feet deep, with a flow of four to five miles per hour.

Willie Condett, like General Fred Walker, could not recall a successful attack across an unfordable river in the face of organized positions. Walker wanted to flank across the river elsewhere—but old Keyes up at Corps said no. Sure, they expected heavy casualties, but it had to be a frontal attack to bring all possible pressure on the Krauts, to protect the Anzio landings. *I hope it's worth it*, Willie thought.

As CO of Mike Company, the Heavy Weapons outfit, he remained with battalion staff. His mortars and heavy machine guns were farmed out with the rifle companies. So he was in a good position to hear what was passed back and forth through the foggy blackness. First Battalion had screwed up from the start.

When they reached their assembly area, they found some of their assault boats already shattered by Kraut artillery fire. Since they now had more men than boat places, they had had to reorganize in the dark. It was a long time before A and B Companies were ready to move out, grunting and cursing, lugging their boats down to the river.

And the dark was no cover now, for the Krauts knew what was coming. Kraut shells shrieked in constantly, and the fog was no help. Stumbling and slipping over the wet ground, B Company went on and on. The men began to tire.

Finally Captain Harmon, the CO, had yelled at the engineer guides, "Where the hell are we going? Where's the river?"

"Jesus, I think we passed the place," the engineers said. "Captain, you'll have to turn the company around—we got to go back some!"

Turning the column in dark and fog and under artillery fire was pure hell.

Men ran into each other, fell down. Then a Kraut concentration whooped in, killing Harmon. His exec cried out with a fragment of steel ripping through him; field jackets were no protection against singing steel. B Company began to flounder helplessly, trying to get organized.

And A Company, a few yards behind, wasn't doing any better. The engineer guides there were lost, too. "Goddamnit, the artillery knocked down all our white guide tapes—we're lost!"

"Well, for Christ's sake keep moving," the Able CO shouted. "We can't stay here in the open!" He pressed forward. "Let's go!"

Blam! The company commander was thrown in the air as he stepped on a mine. He lay groaning, hurt seriously. The exec took over. Now all the men were afraid to move through the unmarked area; the exec tried to raise 1st Battalion HQ on his walkie-talkie. He couldn't get through. Able Company was stranded in the middle of a mine field, under enemy fire.

And 3rd Battalion had to wait until 1st Battalion got the hell out of the way. The confusion at Baker had gone on for hours. Two officers had tried to find a way through the mine fields to the river. No soap. Baker Company huddled miserably against the soggy ground. Not until 0230, four hours later, when Lieutenant Colonel Bird, the battalion commander, came cursing into its area, did it move. Bird took charge and led the company down to the crossing site.

And at the crossing-site itself—*Holy Jesus!* Willie Condett thought. That was the worst of all. The lousy little rubber assault boats they had been issued collapsed like pricked balloons when mortar fragments sprayed the area. The bigger, heavier assault boats were no good either. Not only were the men pooped by the time they got them to the crossing site, but the banks were too steep to launch them. When men leaped into the boats from the high banks, they capsized, and a number of GIs were swept away screaming in the dark, swirling waters.

The Krauts knew precisely where the "S"Bend was, and they kept the shells zinging in. At last, almost miraculously, some of Baker Company reached the west shore. There they met heavy machine-gun fire, and they stopped, digging in. The rest of Baker, without boats, were ordered to wait for an engineer foot bridge to be built.

Now 3rd Battalion moved out; it was growing too late to risk waiting any longer. Moving behind their engineer guides, Willie Condett and the battalion staff heard cries from off to their right. "Help! Get us out of here!" It was Able Company, stuck in the mine field. Quickly, the engineers cleared a path, and the company was attached to 3rd Battalion. Lieutenant Colonel Richardson, the CO, told the acting company commander to join Baker at the crossing site and cross when the first foot bridge was ready.

Coming down to the Rapido, Willie Condett saw the bridge situation was

31

a screaming snafu. Originally four foot bridges had been planned; only the first two assault companies had been issued boats. But one bridge had been found defective in the assembly area and abandoned. A second was blown up in a mine field on the way to the river. Kraut artillery got the third at the flaming hell of the crossing site before it could be erected. The combat engineers, Willie thought, were earning their pay tonight, even if they weren't accomplishing anything so far. Under continuous fire, they finally got the fourth bridge across the river.

"All right, all right! First Battalion across the river!" Lieutenant Colonels Bird and Richardson were trying to untangle their two battalions, get the remnants of A and B across with C Company. By ones and twos men started across the wobbly little bridge, into the inferno of small-arms fire on the west bank.

The bridge was ice-rimed and slippery. Men screamed and fell off, drowning in the deep water. Others made it across on hands and knees. Shell fragments hit a number while on the bridge. And a number of poor bastards reached the far shore, only to step on mines sewn along the bank. Willie Condett felt sick, watching. But all that was left of A and B Companies went across with C. First Battalion had established a bridgehead.

But the Krauts had direct fire from 88s on the crossing now. With a roar, the bridge collapsed and was swept away. *Oh, hell,* Condett thought, *that does it.* The poor suckers over there were cut off.

Now the engineers were trying to put in an eight-ton infantry support bridge, over which 3rd Battalion was supposed to cross. The Kraut artillery blew them out of the water as fast as they laid the sections down. Huddled on the east bank, the 3rd Battalion watched the slow progress with anxious eyes. Condett kept looking to the east. If dawn caught them out here in the open, it would be slaughter.

There was a gigantic roaring, like the sound of a hundred airplane engines. "Tanks! Tanks!" *Pow! Pow! Wheeeeee-bram!* Condett clawed at the dirt, pressing himself deeper as high-velocity shells shrieked over his head. German tanks had moved out of Sant' Angelo across the river and were firing on the crossing site.

Lieutenant Colonel Richardson was down, full of shell splinters. Captain Ford, the battalion S-3, was hit. Major Mehaffey, the exec, took over. He passed Wille Condett, saying, "My God, we've got to get out of here. After daylight we'll be wiped out!"

And at 0530, Mehaffey got permission to pull back. With daylight approaching, there was nothing to do but retreat to the assembly areas, leaving the poor bastards from 1st Battalion isolated across the river.

While 3rd Battalion regrouped, a few wounded men swam back across the river. First Battalion was in trouble. Under the kind of fire it was taking, reorganization was impossible. All commo was out, and the losses among officers and NCOs were disastrous. All 1st Battalion could do now was to hang on, pray that they would be relieved after dark.

And Willie Condett learned that the 143rd, their sister regiment to the south, had been repulsed bloodily also. Only one battalion got across the river, and it was shot to doll rags, forced to return. After a night of vicious combat, the 36th Division had only a few shattered companies across the river.

But this coming night, at 0200, January 22, the troops were going ashore at Anzio. Thirty-sixth Division would have to try again, he knew; the battle of the Rapido was not yet over. After dark, the 141st must try to cross again, to relieve the 1st Battalion and continue the attack.

Captain Willie Condett, meanwhile, did what he could to reorganize M Company, get it ready again for the night's battle. He talked with other battalion officers, listened to the scoop. Six Corps was still out at sea somewhere; this affair on the Rapido would have to continue until they got ashore, at least. General Keyes and General Walker were conferring. They said General Keyes had ordered the 143rd to resume its attack at once—but the 143rd was not moving very fast. Not after what it had taken all night.

And as Willie learned later, when the 143rd finally went across the river again, it met the Panzer Grenadiers head on. Both lead battalions were hurled back across the Rapido, and the supporting battalion never got more than a handful of men across at any time. The 143rd reeled back, forced to retire from action.

But with night, 3rd Battalion of the 141st, with 2nd Battalion now accompanying them, attacked across the river again, to reach their comrades on the west side. This time, the Kraut fire was less vicious. Both battalions made it across, and they found some survivors of the cut-off 1st. By dawn of January 22, all foot elements of the 141st Regiment had crossed the Rapido.

"By God," Mehaffey told Condett, "we're in good shape. Just as soon as they put a bridge in behind us and resupply us, we'll be able to break out and move forward. Maybe tonight."

Fog still hung thickly over the battlefield, but if anything it was more help to the Germans than to 36th. The Krauts knew every inch of the ground; the Americans did not.

But Condett looked up and down the Rapido bank, at the thin lines dug in only a few yards from the river. There was no forward nor rear here; there was no defense in depth. There was only a thin line strung out along the river, 3rd Battalion, and Landry's 2nd Battalion. Something else—half of Willie's own Heavy Weapons Company hadn't made it across, somehow getting lost back there on the river. The battalion had only small arms, mainly, with which to fight. And there was no defilade, no fold of ground for cover.

Ahead, Kraut heavy machine guns had them pinned down completely, and already the intensity of Kraut artillery fire was unbelievable.

So began the second day of the Rapido crossings—a day Willie Condett would never forget. He would be one of the pitifully few Americans who came back from across the river.

On the German side, at XIV Corps HQ, General Fridolin von Senger und Etterlin kept his slender finger on the course of battle. A thin, dark officer, an Oxford graduate who spoke perfect English, Senger also knew any attacking force needed numerical superiority to break through.

During the night, he had moved up the 211th Grenadier Regiment, parts of the 104th Panzer Grenadier—armored infantry—Regiment, and the 115th Reconnaissance Battalion. He could now bring overwhelming strength against the Ami bridgehead. The Liri Valley would earn its name—Purple Heart Valley.

And von Senger ordered the *Führer's* personal message to the troops read to them while they waited in their concrete-lined bunkers, while they sent parties out to remove every twig, every rock, that obscured their fields of fire toward the river.

Hitler told the men manning the *Gustavstellung:* "The *Führer* demands from each man that the line be held to the last. Success may have political repercussions among the Allies." Whatever the aristocratic Fridolin von Senger und Etterlin thought of the *Führer's* rantings, his orders still unquestionably had a good effect on the common soldiers.

And now, with the Americans across the river, the dreaded *Nebelwerfer*, the screaming meemies, began to roar. From their site south of Cassino they could sweep the 141st lines, and in the foxholes along the Rapido-life became pure hell.

Willie Condett saw his platoon sergeant, Sergeant Herron, die from a direct hit on his hole. A little later, Harris, the battalion operations sergeant, was blown to shards the same way. Nobody could move, not even to raise up to fire one of the few mortars they had brought across. And in the fog they couldn't see where to aim anyway. They could only lie in their shallow holes, cursing, waiting for something, anything, to help them out of this.

Condett knew they had a number of green men in the battalion, and he began to worry how the new boys were taking this. In a two-man hole with a raw replacement, he soothed the young man whose jacket had been ripped by shell fragments. "Don't worry—you'll be issued a new one. No statement of charges." It seemed a silly thing to say, he realized, as soon as he said it.

Now the fog was lifting, drifting away—but the artillery and chemical mortar battalion on the American side began firing smoke shells to

34

blanket the bridgehead.

"My God, no!" Captain Condett raved. "The damn idiots are pinpointing our positions!" The American area was so small, the smoke was doing exactly that. And smoke could not deflect the big 88 rounds falling in a constant stream.

Condett crawled along the line of soggy foxholes, touching two men. "Beat it back across the river—tell 'em to lay off that smoke. And tell Divarty to put fire down closer to us." In front, he could hear small-arms fire rattling. The Krauts were beginning to probe the American bridgehead. "Don't be afraid of hitting us—we need close-in fire!" The two men moved out, one at a time. Condett never saw either of them again.

Major Mehaffey now sent a request back for permission to retire. No word came back. The radios were dead, and only voice communication could carry across the river. By midmorning, the engineers were no longer even trying to put in a bridge. Their dead littered the banks of the Rapido, and the fast waters ran red along the muddy shores.

In the spurning, roaring hell of the bridgehead area, it was becoming impossible even to communicate with the man in the next hole. To move was to get hit. A man forty feet away was in a different world. But the two battalions stayed, enduring the constant shelling.

Mehaffey was down now. So was Major Landry of the 2nd Battalion. Every company commander was wounded at least slightly. And the losses among the men in the holes were ghastly. Already, there were more dead and wounded men west of the Rapido than men still able to fight. And then, at 1600, the Krauts attacked.

The gray-green waves ran forward, into a hail of American small-arms fire. It was touch and go for a few minutes as the Germans crawled into the perimeter, but at last they were thrown back, leaving the ground littered with bodies. Half an hour later, they came back.

This time the American fire was less intense. A German officer's nose quivered. After a day of fighting, the Amis were running low on ammunition. He reported back to his regimental HQ. The major commanding the Panzer Grenadiers smiled grimly. The Amis were in the bag; there was no point in wasting men on frontal attacks. But with night, now . . . .

Soon Willie Condett, who seemed to be the only officer capable of organizing the defense, faced a new hazard. Along the points where American and German troops lay close together, English-speaking voices called, "Captain Smith says to surrender! Pass the word! Captain Smith says surrender now!"

"Crap!" Condett bellowed at the men near him. "We haven't got a Captain Smith—nobody surrenders!" He knew there were a number of new men, green replacements, in both battalions. "Get the new men back in with some of the old hands," he ordered. He wanted no panic, no mass sur-

35

renders in the coming dark.

But in a few cases, he was too late. A number of men, both old hands and new, had already taken "Captain Smith's"advice.

Captain Chapin, of E Company, was senior to Willie, but he was hit. He would die before the night was out, and now Captain Dube, commanding 2nd Battalion, came crawling through the dusk. "My God, Condett, what are you going to do?"

"What do you mean, what am I going to do?"

"Hell, man, you're in command of the 3rd, aren't you? Maybe we'd better give up," Dube began, tiredly.

"You can do what you want to, Dube," Condett said. "But I'm not surrendering to no Krauts. A little while ago we got a message yelled across the river—they told us to stay here till we died."

Dube crawled off, and along the perimeter guns continued to flash, and more men died. The Krauts kept probing, and a thin seed of panic began to sprout among the survivors. There was almost no more ammunition.

Willie Condett moved among the 3rd Battalion men, steadying them, trying to get some sort of organization. He would be decorated twice for his actions this night. Somehow, the lines held.

It was hopeless, but they held. There were no orders to retreat. They would stay west of the Rapido until they died.

All day there had been only voice communication across the river, and most of what was passed, under fire, was garbled. On the maps at General Walker's CP, the 36th had almost six battalions across the river. Actually, fewer than one hundred men still survived on the German bank. Keyes, of II Corps, did not think the situation was hopeless, or that he had been defeated. He told Walker to get ready to attack with his reserve regiment, the 142nd.

General Mark Clark returned from the Anzio beachhead late on January 22. His enthusiasm over Lucas' success turned to horror as he was briefed. He advised Keyes to break it off, but he did not actually order the corps commander to halt the battle.

While the higher commanders were talking, someone shouted across the Rapido from the east bank, "Come back! Come back, any way you can II"

Willie Condett recognized a regimental officer's voice. "Move out," he ordered. "Pass the word, quick."

He waited until he felt sure the word had gone around, then he crawled to the icy water and plunged in. He swam across, leaving blood in the water and on the bank. At the east shore, someone handed down a carbine butt, and when he was on dry land again, he took charge of the pitiful remnants of two battalions that were coming across to the American side.

At 2100, Fred Walker was notified that forty-odd men, most of them wounded, had come back across the Rapido. They were all that was left of the three rifle battalions of the 141st. Immediately he telephoned Keyes.

General Keyes, paling, called the battle off. The 142nd would not attack.

Across the river, however, there was still gunfire. A few men had never gotten the word to withdraw. Some men had been too badly hurt to swim the river. The wounded had been abandoned, a bitter thing to Captain Condett. There had been no dignity in retreat. It had been every man for himself—the only way it could be, disorganized, in the dark and under heavy attack. One man had swum back with a foot blown off; he was among the lucky ones. Not until midnight did all firing cease. The last shooting was that of German machine pistols, as the enemy went from hole to hole, taking no chances.

Willie Condett, moving to the shelter of the hills, looked back once. His was a deep and abiding, bitterness. A lot of men, Texans and others, had died for nothing. He was not bitter against the generals. An officer, he knew how the game of war must be played, whether the people back home in Texas did or not. He was not bitter against Keyes or Clark. He was bitter because the 36th had failed.

He was told that night, along with the others, that the terrible losses— 1,681 men—along the Rapido had assured the success of the Anzio landings. Every German reserve had been sucked into the Rapido-Cassino battle, leaving Anzio bare of troops. But this word brought damn little comfort to William Condett, Captain, Infantry, commanding forty survivors of his battalion. He would feel comforted only when he met the enemy again and beat him.

In time, near a place called Anzio, he would.

4

Command Decision

"The strain of a thing like this is a terrible burden. Who the hell wants to be a general?"— General Lucas, on the Anzio beachhead

As Louie Martin's platoon surged through the darkened houses of Anzio, vainly seeking the German enemy, and the veteran 3rd Division pushed in from the beaches south and east of the town, the phones from German command posts in the vicinity of Anzio to Army Group "C"HQ in Rome were snarling. Startled senior officers were pulled from their beds, their heads still muddy from the evening's bottle of Valpolicella or Soave, while their pretty, dark, Italian mistresses cried out shrilly, asking what was happening.

What *was* happening? Nobody knew for sure, except something big was on below Rome. Gradually, as more and more reports in the excited voices of the coast watchers came through, and hot coffee washed away the vestiges of the night's dissipations, the picture grew clearer.

In German eyes, it was a damned bad picture.

But at Army Group "C"Headquarters, quick action was in progress. Someone had told the *Ordannanzoffiziere* of all the generals, and the aides had

38

scurried for their masters. Now the staff officers had to plot the scattered information, and quickly.

"*Schnell! Schnell!* Find the Anzio-Nettuno sheets for the operations map!" The Army Group "C"G.S.O.I, the Operations Officer, was still groggy, though he had been up half an hour, and he was rough-tongued with the enlisted men. This morning of January 22, 1944 the whole staff, except the young duty officer, was groggy and bleary-eyed.

He didn't look so good himself, *Oberfeldwebel* Hannes Dietert thought. Who the hell would, pulled from the sack at 0300?

Dietert snapped at the other enlisted men in the big operations room, with its colored wall maps and humming teletypewriters. "Come on! Snap it up!" Dietert could not remember hearing of Anzio-Nettuno. But they had the map. Army Group "C"staff was thorough.

Obergefreiter Wohl, who had been a schoolteacher before the war, said hesitantly from behind his thin glasses, "Sergeant, here is a Cisterna sheet—"

"Yes, yes," the G.S.0.1 growled, "That is it! Cisterna is near Anzio."

They slapped the sheets up against the boards on the wall and covered them with glassine. "What symbols do we draw?" asked Corporal Wohl.

"Should I know?" Dietert snapped, smoothing his long, blond hair, rubbing sleep from his reddened blue eyes. "All we know is that the Amis have come ashore at Anzio." His young face tightened. "Quiet! Here is the Chief of Staff!"

Major General Siegfried Westphal, big-nosed, square-faced, tired-eyed, strode into the room. "Has the field marshal been notified?" he snapped.

"Yes, *Herr Generalmajor.*"

"Good." Westphal went to the map, studied it carefully, shaking his head. "The very thing Rommel feared, when he was here—a seaborne operation, in our rear . . . ." He stopped muttering, squared his shoulders. Dietert watched him with admiration. Westphal was a tough, competent general—one of the breed Field Marshal Rommel had developed in the Afrika Korps—and like Bayerlein, he had been salvaged from the debacle in North Africa. With Rommel, he had been a lieutenant colonel, but with his ability, promotion had come fast.

Now here came the field marshal—Old Albert—himself. No baton now, and no smile for the troops—Kesselring's jaw was set and determined. There was no panic, no weakness, in the way he stomped up to the map. Dietert sprang to attention with the others.

Westphal said grimly, "The thing we feared back in September—a landing below Rome. I wonder if they have dropped paratroops?"

"None reported," the G.S.0.3, the intelligence officer, said nervously. "At least not yet."

"I would have dropped a division on the Colli Laziali, there," Westphal murmured. "*Mein Gott*, what that would do to us, with all our communications to the south cut !!"

"Well," Kesselring demanded finally, "what have we between Anzio and Rome?"

Westphal shrugged. "Practically nothing, *Herr Feld-marschall*. There are two battalions of the 29th Panzer Grenadier Division on the coast—but we cannot count on them. According to the reports, the Allies have landed at least two divisions, with more to come."

He did not add, *You let von Vietinghoff, the Tenth Army commander, talk you into sending all our reserves in the Rome area to the southern front. Von Senger's XIV Panzer Corps has already committed them along the Garigliano-Rapido. I Parachute Corps, with the 29th and 90th Panzer Grenadier Divisions, are no longer there.* But the look was on his face; even Hannes Dietert recognized it.

Kesselring, big and bluff, but looking harried, met his eyes. "The southern front hung by a slender thread against the Ami Fifth Army attack. But there goes our first plan." Army Group "C"HQ had long feared a landing on the coast near Rome. Plans had been made, but all the plans counted on two mobile divisions and a proper HQ near Rome.

Westphal nodded. "Yes, sir. The Allied landings have a good chance of bringing our main front to a state of collapse because we have no immediate reserves."

Kesselring looked at the hastily thrown together maps. "We must assume that the enemy will seize the Alban Hills, and Highways 6 and 7. This would be the major purpose of any landing." He turned around. "What have you for time, Sergeant?"

"Almost 0500, *Herr Feldmarschall*."

"When did the *Allierte* come ashore?"

"Our estimate is 0200, sir," the G.S.O.1 answered.

"All right," Kesselring said. "Let's see what we can put together. What troops—any kind—are in Rome?"

"The 4th Parachute Division—being activated now."

"New units—green. But one uses what one has," the field marshal murmured. "Have them march on the Colli Laziali, block the approaches west of the hills. What else?"

"The replacement units of the Hermann Göring Panzer Division—"

"Good. Send them, too. They will block from Cisterna."

There was a bustle, and phones buzzed, and hoarse orders went out over the wires. The confusion was quickly brought under control. With officers like Westphal and Kesselring at the helm, there was no panic, no hesitation.

"Now," said Kesselring, smiling wryly, "we must face the inevitable. We tell Berlin." Smiles briefly touched the other faces, as the teletypewriters hummed and clicked. "We might as well spoil the morning for the *Oberkommando der Wehrmacht*, and the *Führer!*"

The OKW, informed, promised help, immediately. At Berlin, also, an

40

Allied landing had been feared, and a plan was in effect. Orders would go at once to the 715th Motorized Infantry Division in southern France, the 114th Light (*Jäger*) Division in Yugoslavia, and every unit in Germany proper which could be put on the road, altogether about one division. A new division, the 92nd Infantry, was to be activated in Italy. But it would be several days before outside help could reach Italy.

"Call Fourteenth Army HQ. They are to give us three divisions."

And so the morning went. At 0710 Fourteenth Army in northern Italy put the following forces at Army Group HQ's disposal: the 65th Division at Genoa (less a regiment), the 362nd Infantry Division (—) at Rimini, and two regiments of the newly formed 16th SS Panzer Grenadier Division. Movement toward Anzio would start with darkness, January 22.

At 0830, Field Marshal Kesselring ordered Tenth Army to transfer a corps HQ to Anzio, plus any combat troops that could be taken from the southern front. Von Vietinghoff, greatly concerned about his rear, pulled I Parachute Corps out of line, and sent all combat troops still in reserve—3rd Panzer Grenadier Division, the 71st Infantry Division, and the Herman Göring Panzer Division.

These units began the race to Anzio at once. From the Adriatic side of the front, von Vietinghoff pledged the 26th Panzer Division and elements of the 1st Parachute Division. But together with von Senger, he strongly advised withdrawal from the southern front, shortening the lines in order to get at least two seasoned divisions to the beachhead.

"No," Kesselring told them, "We gamble." Old Albert, Hannes Dietert thought, listening to the argument that raged around the CP, had courage. "If the Allies do not move for two or three days, we can contain them. So far, they have only gone ashore—they are not pushing far inland, as we expected."

Behind him, Westphal's mouth turned down. "If they attack tomorrow, or on the twenty-fourth, we won't stop them," he said softly.

"But if they do not attack strongly by the twenty-fourth, then we shall have divisions from Tenth Army front at Anzio," Kesselring said, tracing lines on the map with his fingers. "It is a good gamble. If we pull back in the south, as Vietinghoff wants, we risk disaster."

Young Sergeant Dietert felt a quick thrill of pride for the courageous, competent manner in which his superiors took action against the Allied threat. This was a German staff! No panic, no confusion, but decisions made firmly and quickly. And no fear of a gamble, if the rewards seemed high enough.

Later, after the war, *Oberfeldwebel* Dietert would remember this day, and he would compare it with later days in Italy, when the *Führer* himself sent furious orders. He would compare the days, and the orders, and even a mere staff sergeant could have his own ideas as to how the war was lost.

41

"Well, that does it," Westphal said, softly. "We have done what we can. Now it is up to the generals over there. I wonder who is commanding at Anzio? Does he know a quick move across our communications would lead to victory? If he has troops enough . . ."

Wohl and Dietert looked at each other. They were thinking the same thing. It had been pleasant, being stationed in Rome, and they had no desire to leave. For a number of hours, perhaps days, the road to Rome would be open.

Oberfeldwebel Dietert was thinking, would the *verdammte Allierte* gamble, too?

While Field Marshal Albert Kesselring was making his command decision not to withdraw the German armies in the south, but to contain the beachhead at Anzio, a few miles south of Rome *Rittmeister* Edwin Wentz was up early. There wasn't much to do here in the replacement companies of the Hermann Göring Division for an over-age captain of cavalry detailed to the division, but there had been a lot of firing over toward the coast during the night, and in the dawn there seemed to be a thousand of the damned American planes aloft.

Gott sei dank, the planes were flying on somewhere else, probably plastering the air fields closer to Rome. The Amis weren't interested in the replacement training units of the Hermann Göring Division outside of Cisterna and a fifty-year-old *Rittmeister* retread from the last war, drinking *ersatz* coffee and feeling both his years and the humid Italian winter in his bones.

"*Fernsprecher, Herr Rittmeister*," Wentz' orderly, Pomerantz, said. "A Herr Major Weil, from Rome, I think."

Wentz took the phone unhappily. Now what, so early in the morning? "Herr Major?"

"Wentz? Do you know the Amis have landed near Anzio?"

"*Herr Gott!*" Wentz said. "That is only twelve kilometers from here!"

"You must take charge of all troops in your area, move them into Cisterna at once. You must block off every road leading to Highway 6 and 7. Do you understand me, Captain?"

"I understand." *My God*, Wentz thought, *what troops? My green replacements?*

"Take every man fit for duty in the replacement depot," Weil said, anticipating his question. "And there will be other units and individual soldiers falling back from the coast. We had some Panzer Grenadiers on the beach; no one knows what happened to them, but some must have gotten away. We are sending you reconnaissance troops, convalescents, anything we can scrape up. You will assume command of these, Captain, organize them into a provisional battalion, or battle group, and you will block all enemy attack to the east, toward Cisterna."

"*Prima*," Wentz said. "Splendid! Would it be too much to ask for a few provisional guns and tanks, too, assuming the Allied attack is not provisional?"

There was silence at the other end of the wire. Wentz looked up, saw Pomerantz, quick grin wiped away. "My dear Wentz," the major said sharply, "someday that tongue of yours will get you into trouble. Stop joking now, and to, work!"

"*Jawohl*," Edwin Wentz said. He placed the phone down and gravely saluted it. "Pomerantz!"

"*Herr Rittmeister?*"

"We are now *Kampfgruppe Wentz*, and we are going to Cisterna to fight an Allied invasion." Wentz passed a weathered hand over his bald head. "Get the sergeants, that's a good fellow."

Pomerantz ran out. The poor chap probably thought his officer was crazy, Wentz thought sadly. Why not—everybody was crazy these days. And try as he might, Edwin Wentz had not been able to bring to war the attitude of the typical professional German officer. To German officers, war was never laughable, rarely tragic. They approached it with a fervor that the English reserved only for sport, or the Americans for the big business deal.

Wentz' hand went down to touch the old belt buckle he wore. On it was inscribed *Ehre*, just as on his sword, packed away back home. *Honor.* But you didn't need that in a war any more; like swords, it had passed from use. Honor, and swords, and "good"regiments were gone forever.

Rittmeister Wentz had once belonged to a good Hannoverian regiment long ago, in another war. Now there were elite troops, but no good regiments. And many officers were ruffians, pretending, with their stars, that they were gentlemen.

In the dawn, *Rittmeister* Edwin Wentz felt a sudden chill. If Germany won this war, the day of the ruffians was assured, a thing he found hard to contemplate. If she lost—but that, too, was unthinkable. For this time her enemies would destroy her. All a man could do was fight, and hope for the best.

"*Befehl ist befehl,*" Edwin Wentz murmured. "Orders are orders." But perhaps, this one time, near Cisterna he might find honor once again.

And as Louie Martin's platoon moved cautiously inland, looking for trouble, while the phones were jangling and buzzing in Rome, Major General John P. Lucas stood at his command post on the bridge of the cruiser *Biscayne*, looking toward the beaches of Anzio with unbelieving eyes.

In the early dawn no red and white tracers were flying. There was no hollow booming of artillery, no corpses littering the beaches, no lines of wounded streaming back to the hospital ships.

The unbelievable had happened. The Anzio landings had achieved complete surprise.

It was incredible, Lucas thought. Of all the things he had expected to happen, this was not one of them. In modern warfare, this just didn't happen!

But by daylight, most of the foot elements of VI Corps had gone ashore. And as the long morning wore on, the fantastic good luck continued. By 0900 General. Truscott reported the 3rd Division firmly established on the beachhead line, which Lucas had hoped they would reach by dark of the twenty-second. The only opposition that counted was an air raid just after 0600. Of course, the Ranger force had pushed far inland, and with characteristic bravado had routed out a few Huns. But that was all.

Now Lucas began to think ahead. There was German armor, German grenadiers, back there in that brooding, low-lying hill mass called the Colli Laziali. There had to be! Six Corps had gotten a break—but now it was going to be a question of how fast they could unload supplies and build up the beachhead.

When it became apparent that there was no German opposition on the beaches, Lucas thought fleetingly of sending a regimental combat team on to the hills. But he did not seriously consider this very long. He expected the German reaction at any minute, and when it came, it would be vicious. No, it was too risky to send troops ranging far inland across the German lines of communications, and besides, his orders didn't read that way. General Clark had left it up to him—everyone understood that.

Lucas decided he would advance on the Colli Laziali only when the beaches were completely secure and he had overwhelming strength ashore. If the enemy caught him half on, half off—Lucas shook his head, firm in his belief that rashness now would only result in the loss of his entire corps.

About midmorning, when his five thousand vehicles were rolling over the beaches, Lucas himself went ashore from the *Biscayne*. He found Lucian Truscott's CP in a small wood a few hundred yards back from the sea. The 3rd Division commander's cook, Private Hong, was cooking breakfast for Truscott and his chief of staff, Colonel Carlton. And Mark Clark, and his Operations Officer, Don Brann, in by PT boat, were busily eating. The hood of Truscott's command, jeep was littered with tin mess plates.

"By god, fresh eggs!" Lucas said. "Where the devil did that Chinaman get those? Sure, I'd love some."

Then Lucas reported to Clark. General Clark was quite pleased with the success of the landing, but he seemed somewhat subdued. Lucas guessed he was depressed by the events that had occurred along the Rapido River; down there the 36th Division was getting the hell stomped out of them. Clark had always been a worrier about public opinion, Lucas thought, and the way the Texas Division was getting shot up, he might have something to worry about.

But Clark said General Alexander was pleased, too, about the way things were turning out, and very optimistic about the whole operation.

Lucas told Clark, "Getting the port of Anzio intact, ready to go into

44

immediate operation, is going to be our salvation. To keep it operative, I am going to supervise personally setting up an antiaircraft warning system, build an air field, and clear this clutter of supplies coming ashore off the beaches. This is, in the long run, going to be a logistical battle between ourselves and the Huns."

Clark agreed, but he did tell Lucas that he should push in a little more, perhaps throw a few troops into Cisterna, to take that important center from the Germans. Scouts who had gone out claimed the whole area was devoid of enemy; a group of artillery officers had walked almost into the outskirts of the town. But Clark's mind was on the Rapido battle going so badly in the south. He felt there could be no quick link-up between VI Corps and the main body of Fifth Army.

"You can forget this goddamn Rome thing, Johnny," he said. "Don't stick your neck out. I did at Salerno and got into trouble." Clark got up, prepared to go back to Naples.

Lucas shook hands with him, saluted. Johnny Lucas was not about to stick his neck out. This was the most important job he would ever do, and he would not be stampeded.

To Johnny Lucas, it seemed downright imprudent to strike off immediately for the Alban Hills. *Damnit, he was not going to risk losing his whole corps. Clark and Alexander had left him free to choose, and he was going to choose the wisest course. After all, there was never a big breakthrough except in the story books. . . .*

To hell with Rome. Perhaps they would criticize him as over-cautious, but a general who lost his men was worse than reckless, he was criminal. If Sir Harold Alexander wanted more than the port of Anzio taken, then he should have given Lucas bigger forces, enough to do the job. When those two German divisions up near Rome attacked now, if he had his lines extended, all strung out twenty miles inland to the Colli Laviali . . .

A commander makes a decision basically by ruling out all opposing courses of action. This is how Major General Johnny Lucas solved his problem: he rejected all courses of action that seemed reckless or unwise. Securing the beachhead and clearing the port of Anzio seemed to come first. After that, he would order the advance on the Alban Hills. . . .

Thus, while Field Marshal Kesselring and Army Group "C" staff sweated and threw together a "higgledy-piggledy jumble of units," as Kesselring called it, wondering how the American advance could be stopped without troops, the American troops were not moving. It would be seven days before General Lucas would be prepared to mount his offensive to the east.

From France, from Germany, from Yugoslavia, and other parts of Italy, *Wehrmacht* divisions were already on the move. Although on January 22, 1944 General Lucas could not know it, by the time the beaches were secure and the port of Anzio clear, it might be much too late to move at all.

Part Two

Bloodletting

A major move to decide the war in Italy had begun. The Allies had landed 50,000 men behind the, German lines; soon the number would increase to over 100,000. The surprise had been complete. U.S.VI Corps was in the German rear.

But the German had reacted vigorously and courageously, in accordance with prior planning to meet such a threat. That he was skillful, both in build-up and defense, would be an understatement. He had been surprised, but not, as Winston Churchill had hoped, frightened.

Now, on the beaches, General Lucas of VI Corps had made his decision: to secure the port and build up his supplies before risking a dangerous push inland. This decision he made for what seemed to him good and sufficient reason. It must be remembered that the Anzio assault was not an all-out attack, with overwhelming force. It was always what Mark Clark called it, a dangerous gamble, a calculated risk.

And Field Marshal Kesselring had made his decision: there would be no pull-back on the southern front. New forces would be assembled, or brought in from elsewhere, to stem the Allied tide. First, he would try to contain the beachhead; then he would—must—try to destroy it. Its threat to his communications was very real.

For seven days each side would skirmish, feel the other out, try to build up its strength. Then, on the eighth day, the agony of Anzio would begin. . . .

5

Six Came Back

"It was a halfway measure as an offensive that was your basic error."—Field Marshal Albert Kesselring to AP Correspondent Daniel De Luce, January, 1946, referring to Allied failures at Anzio

Lieutenant Louie. Martin returned to his Ranger platoon with a bright seed of excitement sprouting within him.

"All right, men," he said, as his platoon gathered around him, "we are going to move out. This is the big attack."

Seven days on the beachhead had not been easy for Martin or the platoon. The second day, they had pushed inland seven miles, and then they had helped hold the line in the Carroceto-Aprilia area. They had met Krauts, not many of them, but all had fought fanatically. For several days, there had been bitter, bloody skirmishing in the rain and many men had died.

Martin felt that during the first few days they could have gone to Rome, if they had been ordered to do so. But the big push all along the beachhead wasn't ready. The Rangers couldn't do it all alone.

And the Krauts seemed to be getting tougher all the time!

Already, Martin hated Anzio. Anzio wasn't the kind of place a man grew fond of. First, there was the weather. On January 26, it began to rain and sleet, and now the ground was sopping wet everywhere. Second, there were German air raids. The *Luftwaffe* was supposed to be finished—but German planes roared over the beachhead day and night, most often at dusk, when Allied air cover had to depart for their distant bases. On one raid alone, Louie Martin counted over two hundred German planes.

God, what a mess! The bombs whistled down, bursting redly, shaking the soggy ground. Trucks overturned, ammo dumps exploding, dead men everywhere, fires blazing all over the port area. The beachhead was only about fifteen miles wide and less than ten deep, and it was crawling with men and vehicles. It didn't matter where the lousy Krauts dropped their stuff—somebody got it in the ass.

The Kraut artillery were bringing up more guns every day. Again, it didn't matter where they aimed; they could let fly anywhere at the beachhead area, and it was fifty-fifty they'd scrag somebody.

To Louie Martin this sitting still, this waiting, while ever more men and supplies piled ashore, made no sense. The thing to do was to push the Kraut, keep him off balance. And to move out and take those damned hills over there—the Colli Watchacallit. From them the Kraut could look down their throats.

What was it the Infantry School said? Do *something*, even if it's wrong!

Now, the 1st Armored Division had put two combat commands ashore, and most of the 45th Division had landed. Martin's battalion commander, Major Dobson, had told Louie that General Truscott, limping on a bad leg—the result of an air raid—and wheezing from laryngitis, had been pecking at Lucas day and night to get started. The 3rd Division's rifle battalions had not been completely idle. They had been pushing slowly ahead, and the going was getting a little tougher each day. There seemed to be fanatical German resistance along the whole line. Not many troops on the other side yet, but they were fighting stubbornly.

Louie Martin had wondered a couple of times whether anyone had worried whether the Germans were getting stronger, too, while all this waiting was going on. The only way to break out now, after letting the Kraut gather strength for seven days, was a big push all along the perimeter. Truscott had been ready, but 3rd Division, even with the Rangers attached, couldn't do it without support. But General Lucas kept holding off for one more day.

Now, at last, the big push had been approved. At 0100, January 30, 1944, the VI Corps attack would jump off. And the Rangers would lead the way.

"Okay, men, here's the general picture," Louie said as his men crowded around. "General Penney's British will make a main effort up the Albano Road to seize the road center at Campoleone. Then General Harmon will shoot a combat command from the 1st Armored around to the left and attack the

Alban Hills from the west.

"The Thunderbird boys—the 45th—are going to relieve elements of the 3rd Division and the British along the flanks. Corps engineers, too, will be on line, to release more troops for the main effort. Now, 3rd Division and the Five-o-four Paratroops will make a frontal attack toward Cisterna, take it, then cut Highway 7 and advance toward Velletri. Got it?"

"What do we do while all this is going on, sir?" Krueger asked dourly.

Martin grinned. "One hour before the 3rd jumps off, 1st and 3rd Rangers will infiltrate through the Kraut lines in front of Cisterna. Two battalions, almost eight hundred men. The 4th Battalion will follow us later. We go into Cisterna in the dark, raise all the hell we can, until the 3rd Division breaks through and joins us."

Around the platoon there were grim, silent nods. This was the kind of work the Rangers had been trained to do. Snoop and poop, night work, then street fighting, hitting the enemy with everything they had. Three battalions of Rangers behind the Kraut lines could blow the whole front open.

"We shouldn't have too much trouble getting past the Kraut lines," Louie continued. "Our recon shows that we face elements of the Nazi Hermann Göring Division, and they're scattered all over hell and gone. All they've got is a mobile defense, with scattered strong points here and there. No solid line. The setup is made for our kind of operation."

Again the faces nodded. Meyer, Henry, Pella, the quiet Krueger—their initial buck fever of the day of landing was gone now. *As nice a bunch of hired killers as I ever saw,* Louie Martin thought. *And we'll be in the thick of it. After the war, they'll never have to ask: "Where were you?"*

Around midnight of the twenty-ninth, the Ranger battalions were moving out. Faces blackened, carrying knives and light arms, and as little ammunition and metal as possible to hold down the noise, they looked like a bunch of pirates in the dark, Louie thought.

Coming up to the forward American outposts along the Corps Beach-head Line, the battalions dispersed. They couldn't cross in large numbers. It would have to be by squads, even individuals, in places, reassembling at predesignated points later.

The front was quiet, only occasional harassing and interdictory fire from the opposing artillery slamming away. Looking over the flat ground to the front, Louie Martin was glad the night was inky, overcast. He wouldn't want to do this under a full moon.

Now the scouts went ahead, stealthily. They had the dirty work—polishing off the sentries and listening posts along the way. It was the sort of work Louie Martin didn't care for, but the officer leading the way, Jim Fowler, ate it up. Lieutenant Fowler would have done well in the old days. Martin waited the proper time, then moved forward, crawling over the sodden, marshy ground.

Once, well into the German lines, he came across an outpost with two slumped forms in gray-green overcoats. He didn't bother to investigate. Fowler and his boys had done their work well.

Now he was reassembling his platoon, bringing them together. "Where the hell's Pella?" he asked, missing the familiar face.

Pella was lost somewhere back there. "Hell with him. Let's move on," Louie said. Pella would probably catch up later. If not—Louie shook his shoulders. There was going to be more than one Ranger scragged this night. This operation wasn't going to be a repeat of D-Day.

Off in the dark they saw farmhouses looming up silently. They must be full of Krauts. They moved on, quietly, undetected. A scout crawled back.

"Hold it," he whispered. "Must be a Kraut battery up ahead. I can see gun emplacements, men around them talking Kraut."

"We'll have to go around them. Can't stop," Martin said. Scouting off to their right, someone found an irrigation ditch. The ditch held knee-deep water, and it was icy.

"In the ditch," Martin snapped. "One at a time. Keep low. Crawl past those positions up ahead."

He slipped into the numbing water of the ditch, sucked in his breath. When he was a kid, he used to get sore throats each time he got his feet wet. He hoped he wouldn't get one now—then he found himself smiling. It was an effort to keep from giggling out loud. By God, he'd settle for a sore throat tonight, and gladly!

At last, sodden, slimy, shivering, he crawled back out of the ditch, watching the dark forms of his men loom up around him. "Meyer, put that goddamn grenade away," he ordered. "You know the colonel's orders—want to give this show away?"

"They'd never know what hit 'em, sir," Meyer muttered. But he put the grenade away.

Now the battalions were linking up, coming back together again. This far behind German lines it was safer to stay in large units, ready to fight if they were detected. They were close to Cisterna now. Both 1st and 3rd Battalions had made it across the lines intact. Fourth Battalion should be somewhere behind them, and off to the left. Major Dobson was elated. When they linked with the 4th, they would have a passel of Krauts caught in a trap, encircled. But the orders said go into Cisterna, and the battalions went forward.

Major Miller's 3rd Battalion had a bad scare crossing one of the built-up roads in the area. Just as they started to cross in a body, Kraut armored cars came roaring out of the dark, no lights showing.

The Rangers hit the ground on either side of the road. Vehicle after vehicle followed down the road, personnel carriers and finally tanks. Alvah Miller felt a gnawing of worry at his mind—where the devil was all this Kraut armor coming from? Was the Hermann Göring Division holding night maneuvers?

He jumped up. "All right, cross in sections, between vehicles. They'll never see you." To show what he meant, he dashed across the road in front of a buttoned-up tank. The entire 3rd followed his example successfully.

Louie Martin looked at his watch, realized it was almost dawn. Behind them the front had begun to blaze with artillery and small arms. Third Division was pushing ahead and from the sound of things they were hitting a stone wall. The firing swelled, but to Martin's ear the front was not moving.

Whispered words were passed back along the line. "Kraut bivouac ahead. Krauts sleeping on the ground. Whole company—"

Their orders were not to fight until they reached Cisterna—but the inevitable happened. In the German bivouac a man called out sharply.

"Wer da? Who goes there?"

"Let 'em have it!" Louie screamed. He snapped a shot at the running sentry, saw the man fall. All around him the rifles and Thompson submachine guns roared, as a hail of bullets laced the surprised. Germans. The Rangers charged forward, yelling like banshees, shooting and slashing with bayonets.

Surprised in their sleep, the Krauts had no chance at all.

A German soldier ran out from behind the trees, crashed into Martin in the dark. Martin pushed him back, tried to lift his carbine. Before he could fire, Meyer used the bayonet, swiftly, viciously. It was a rough war.

Rangers and Germans floundered about on the ground. There were shouts and screams as the Ranger knives found flesh. And suddenly there were no more Germans. The company had been wiped out.

But a few men escaped, running for their lives down the road to Cisterna.

"Regroup! Regroup!" Martin snapped. "Let's go!" The Ranger companies came together again, moving past the grisly bivouac area. There was no time to waste. The town of Cisterna was only a few hundred yards ahead, and the Rangers were in open fields, with light just breaking.

It was here that all hell broke loose.

While the Ranger battalions were infiltrating the widely scattered strong points of the Herman Göring Division, *Rittmeister* Edwin Wentz was having a bad night. This was no change; he had not had a good night's rest since January 22, the day the Allies landed.

Now, in his command post in Cisterna, he listened to the sound of firing to the west and thought, *No sleep tonight*. Then he studied his watch. Only an hour till dawn, anyway, and an old man needed little sleep.

But an old man needed rest, and there was precious little of that. Even his troops, these eighteen-year-old replacements, were dead tired.

For seven days, *Rittmeister* Wentz had fought with his provisional battalion, formed from replacements, convalescents, fragments fleeing from the coast.

It had been a terrible seven days. Those *verdammten* veterans of the 3rd Division had chopped his men to pieces—but they had not pushed the attack for the first few days. That had been his salvation. For each day, more German men and units arrived.

Wentz was no longer in command of the operation. General Eberhard von Mackensen's Fourteenth Army had been sent from North Italy to command the beachhead battle. A semblance of organization had come to the German forces, though they were still fighting with a profusion of units, in bits and pieces. If the Allied did not start their big offensive, there was a chance, Wentz realized, that the lines could hold. Hour by hour the German situation improved. When the tough divisions arrived from von Vietinghoff's southern front . . .

A sergeant entered with impeccable salute. In the past few days, Wentz, sergeants had ceased to laugh at *Der Alte*. "*Herr Rittmeister*, an officer from the 26th Panzer Division—"

Twenty-sixth Panzer! The veteran troops from the southern front were arriving! Wentz stepped into the next room of his CP and took the young lieutenant's crisp salute.

"Good morning, sir. We have an armored column coming up the road. Can you direct me?"

"Thank God," Wentz breathed. "Our division front is very thin, Lieutenant. More than twenty miles, little armor, little artillery. You have come in time!"

The young liaison officer explained the 26th Panzer had orders to move into line north of Cisterna. Quickly, from his map, Wentz showed the officer the area and routes. The Panzer lieutenant clicked heels, saluted, and was off.

Within minutes the darkness before the dawn was filled with the wonderful roaring of tank engines. The big monsters roared through Cisterna, shaking the old stone walls.

Now the phone was buzzing. Wentz belted on his pistol and put his heavy stahlhelm over the long-billed gray cap on his head. Feeling a little like an elongated scarecrow in the big helmet, he took up the phone.

The commander of the SS Regiment on Wentz' right was on the wire. "Something is rotten in Denmark," the heavy, Baltic voice of the SS *Obersturmbannführer* snapped. "Some of the men in our listening posts have been killed—throats cut. The Amis are pushing along the whole line. We may have been infiltrated. Be alert!"

"*Natürlich, Herr Obersturmbannführer*," Wentz croaked.

He hung up. He despised the SS. He was thinking of a saying he had

54

heard recently: the Reich was fighting the war with a Royal Prussian Army, an Imperial German Navy and a Nazi Air Force. There was more than a little truth to that. The Army and the Navy had some traditions, while the Air Force was a Nazi creation. But the *Schutzstaffel!* If Wentz had to describe the SS, the only word he could think of was *swine*. They were scum, if they were older men; if they were young lads, they were the children whom the regime had corrupted completely. Fanatics, too, all of them.

The phone was leaping again. *Enemy soldiers in the fields outside Cisterna! A sleeping company wiped out!*

Wentz put down the phone, shouted, "Get that Panzer officer back here!" The Amis thought they had infiltrated one under-strength, overextended division. They were in for a surprise.

The young Panzer lieutenant dashed in, bringing a major with him. Quickly they conferred with Wentz. Then he called, coordinating with the artillery and the mortars. Finally, Wentz asked for some of the division flak wagons to be moved forward. The 20-mm. flak wagon, it had been originally designed for antiaircraft use, could go over the ground like a vacuum cleaner, chewing up everything in front of it. Then he went forward, quickly, to see what was happening in front of the town.

From a stone house he had a good view of the open fields around Cisterna. There—there, something was moving through the marshy plain. A file of soldiers—and in OD, not field green!

"Pass the word to open fire," *Rittmeister* Wentz said calmly.

To Louie Martin, everything seemed to open up at once. Tracers burned through the air; mortars *crump-crumped* in sudden showers. Fire blossomed through the wet fields, from stone houses, from entrenchments dug before Cisterna, from tanks hidden behind haystacks. Two of his men were down, scrabbling in the mud. The rest of his platoon, with the bulk of both battalions, were strung out along a series of irrigation ditches.

In the open it was slaughter. "Dig in—dig in!" the order came.

Swiftly, Martin's men dug into the wet ground along the ditch banks. In shallow holes, they returned fire for fire. Martin was not worried—hell, he had known they'd have to fight for Cisterna. But soon the 4th Rangers would come up from the rear, and the 3rd Division's attack would be rolling into Cisterna from the flank.

But this was not to be. Moving out one day later than the 1st and 3rd Battalions, the 4th Ranger Battalion had advanced less than half a mile when it was fired upon. Machine-gun tracers stabbed out of the night, men dropped. The leading company attacked, hurling grenades, slashing in with bayonets. Quickly, two machine-gun nests were overrun. But behind these, more guns opened up.

55

Fourth Battalion had run into a strong point in the German line, organized in depth!

Lieutenant George Nunnelly, the leading company commander, ordered two violent assaults against the strong point. During the second attack he was killed. The Krauts had set their automatic weapons to pour grazing fire over the ground in front of them, and every inch was covered by a hail of machine-gun bullets. The remnants of the company took cover in a shallow ditch.

Desperately, the 4th's CO, Colonel Murray, ordered A and B Companies to advance on the right flank. They ran into a vicious fusillade of fire and steel and two more company commanders died. The Rangers were forced to halt, while the fire fight raged with mounting intensity.

Colonel Darby was with the 4th Rangers. In radio contact with the two units in front of Cisterna, he knew these were stopped, and that the 4th must break through. Blue eyes narrowed, his ruddy, clear-skinned face tense, Darby ordered the 4th to move forward. He kept his command post with the forward battalion lines.

The battalion moved forward now, but with frightful losses. One platoon lost a lieutenant, four NCOs, and five men attacking a machine-gun nest. German machine guns were everywhere, and German mortars spat a rain of death into the Ranger ranks. A German paratroop battalion had moved up to block the way. On Darby's staff, Major Bill Martin died, killed by mortar shards. Darby's personal runner, Corporal Stroud, was killed seconds later.

Worried now, Darby called on the 3rd Division and the 504th Parachute Infantry. But these units had troubles equal to the Rangers'. All along the front, the American attack was stalled.

The Rangers who had infiltrated through to Cisterna were trapped.

As morning deepened, and the German fire increased in tempo, Louie Martin began to realize something was wrong. The Rangers here were being cut to pieces; help did not come, and the Germans seemed to be much stronger than anyone had suspected.

A Kraut flak wagon rumbled down a road now, depressing its guns, blazing away at the Rangers in their shallow holes. Angrily, Martin fired his futile carbine at the lumbering monster, while a hailstorm of metal churned the earth about him.

Blam! Suddenly, the flak wagon exploded, throwing the bodies of its crew into the air. A Ranger mortar crew had put its weapon together coolly under fire and was firing with deadly accuracy. The flak wagon slewed, ran into the ditch where it remained, smoking.

But tanks and SPs from the German side were getting into the fight now, and mortar shells couldn't stop those armored behemoths. Martin saw Major Alvah Miller run forward, charging a heavy tank at the head of his men. The tank gun flamed with an ear-splitting crash. Alvah Miller never knew what killed him.

"God, we need artillery!" Krueger panted, crawling up beside Martin. "Sir, can't you get through?"

"No way to direct it," Louie Martin snapped. "They don't know where we are, and we can't tell them, exactly." The dread guns of the 3rd Division Divarty, which could have helped so much, were helpless to prevent the continuing Ranger blood bath.

Part of a Ranger company had found cover in an irrigation ditch. But the Krauts had smelled them out, and three SP guns, their long 77-mm. snouts waving like the heads of serpents, straddled the ditch, firing point-blank at the American troops.

Fighting desperately but coolly, the men in the ditch destroyed all three armored self-propelled guns with rocket launchers. The bazooka shells blasted into the SPs, left them burning. A fourth SP gun tried to move up the ditch, but its way was blocked by the burning hulks. It depressed its vicious 77-mm. cannon to fire into the crowded ditch.

Before it could fire, a lone Ranger crawled up under it and slammed a sticky AT grenade to its underside. Then the Ranger slid away. The SP gun blew up like a rotten tin can.

But the Rangers were under heavy fire from all four directions now. More and more tanks, hampered only by the wet ground, moved up to fire into the bloody fields. On the right, the black uniforms of the SS could be seen coming closer, and from Cisterna the entrenched Krauts kept up a killing fire.

A Kraut machine gun was moved up close to Martin's platoon. The MG 42 began to snarl in sharp, vicious bursts. Martin heard one of his men—he thought it was Henry—scream as steel ripped his throat. He hugged his hole and cursed.

They didn't have the chance of a snowball in hell!

Out in the middle of a field, a Ranger officer was trying to rally his shattered battalion. Major Dodson knew he was cut, off; there was no going back. The only hope for the Rangers was to move into Cisterna.

He stood up, waving his scattered forces forward. "Let's go! Let's go!"

Martin ran forward, leading his remaining men. His platoon did not succumb to Panzer fever. *Whoosh!* Someone fired a bazooka at the Mark IV Panther behind a haystack. *Blam!* Both hay and tank went up in a sheet of flame.

But a monster Tiger blocked Martin's way, and no 2.36 bazooka would penetrate its turret armor. Louie leaped frantically to one side as the Tiger's machine gun opened up, sprayed bullets through the open pistol port on the tank's turret. Then Krueger was on the rear sponson of the tank, a grenade cocked in his hand. Before the tank commander could close the hatch, the grenade bounced in.

Louie Martin could hear the screams of the tank crew before the tank blew.

The Rangers finished several tanks that way, but it was hopeless. As. Major Dobson came up beside the Tiger Martin's men had knocked out, he was wounded seriously. So far as Martin could tell, every company commander with the two battalions had already been killed.

Under increasing fire, and more tanks, the Ranger attack broke up. Yet the Ranger survivors huddled in small pockets, still fighting, still dangerous.

Martin charged a machine gun that was pinning his men down. As he leaped toward it, a slug shattered his carbine, tearing it from his hand. He drew his pistol and threw a grenade. *Pow!* The Krauts staggered back from the upturned gun, and with the .45 automatic he shot two of them.

Rrripp! Rrripp! Steel tore at him from two more machine guns, furrowing the wet earth behind him. Desperately, to save his life, he hit the dirt. Somehow, he broke his GI glasses.

Goddamn! He couldn't see a thing without those glasses! Blindly, he scrambled about, trying to find a hole.

He heard Germans on either side of him and sucked in his breath. Then he felt the brutal jab of a gun barrel in his back, heard the harsh command. Why they didn't shoot, he'd never know. He got to his feet, slowly.

Louie Martin surrendered. There was nothing else to do.

Now, for the Rangers, the end came swiftly. They had had only the cartridges in their belts, and they were out of ammo. Though they fought on with captured guns, there was no way to halt the German tanks. Behind them, the SS, Panzer Grenadiers and *Fallschirmjäger* —paratroopers— were attacking viciously. The huge Mark VIs lumbered along the irrigation ditches, straddling them, their roaring and clanking approach enough to strike terror to the bravest heart. The 88-mm.s, depressed, blew Rangers out of the dirty water. Behind the tanks, the SS advanced, shooting and bayoneting the wounded, quickly, unemotionally.

The SS fought a rough war, too.

By midmorning, the Ranger pocket was very small. Some men had only knives or bayonets. Eight men of Martin's platoon joined him in captivity. The rest were dead or wounded, lying in the ditches, still under fire.

Just before noon, the sergeant major of the 1st Battalion radioed back to Colonel Darby for the last time. "They're closing in on us, Colonel. We're out of ammo—but they won't get us cheap! Colonel . . . good luck!"

At his CP. William Darby asked his staff to leave. He did not want them to see the tears in his eyes. Darby's Rangers had been destroyed.

Of the two battalions which reached Cisterna—767 officers and men— six men came back.

58

6

Lance the Abscess South of Rome!

"Lance the abscess south of Rome!"—Hitler's personal order to Field Marshal Albert Kesselàing

0100, January 30, 1944, VI Corps had begun its massive offensive to break out of the Anzio beachhead. By 1200, January 30, the Ranger Force had been destroyed as a fighting unit. On the southern end of the beachhead line nothing was going as planned. With the Ranger infiltration pinched off, 3rd Division had to attack frontally across open fields, into fields of fire carefully prepared by the German defenders, who hourly grew in number. Third Division continued the attack with great gallantry, trying to enter Cisterna.

It was slow going. For every foot of earth, there was a price to pay in blood. It was grinding infantry warfare at its worst.

Meanwhile, to the north of the 3rd Division front, General Penney's British division, supported by the American 1st Armored, was attempting to break out through the town of Campoleone and flank the Colli Laziali. And, unfortunately, the British and 1st Armored had their troubles, too.

PFC Kenneth Hurley, loader in Tuck's 1st Light Tank Battalion, 1st Armored Division, was a young man of philosophical nature, which was

59

marred only by a violent Irish temper. Right now, like most of the men in the 1st Armored, he knew everything was screwed up. He didn't mind too much, since nobody could blame a dam PFC for this mess.

All they could do was get him killed.

Now, in the early morning hours of January 31, waiting to jump off again against the stubborn Kraut resistance he reviewed the troubles of the past two days. Old Ironsides had come ashore at Anzio, and its armor-plated firepower was supposed to be the edge that would blast the Krauts loose from their positions along the Anzio-Albano road, cut a swath through to the Alban Hills. The generals had looked at their maps. An armored attack northwest from the beachhead along the Anzio-Albano highway to Campoleone, then an end run, flanking the hill mass, seemed in order.

There was only one thing wrong.

The maps didn't show it, but the ground was untankable off the paved roads. The flat areas were sopping wet from the rain and soft as molasses, and the rest of the ground was cut gullies and ravines. Every time the 1st Armored Division tried to maneuver, *squish-squunk!*—stuck in the mud. Then it took hours, sometimes under artillery fire, to winch the heavy vehicles back onto firm ground.

There were plenty of good roads all through the area. But there was one catch to using them. The Krauts had mined them, and they had placed AT guns, both 77s and 88s, about every ten feet. Ken Hurley was thinking, *Unless we find out how to put wings on these goddamn scows, we'll go nowhere far today.*

The first day, the 1st Armored had sent a reconnaissance in force to mark the way and hold the line of departure for the main attack on January 30. Combat Command A, under Colonel Kent Lambert, was to pass through the British 1 Division once the Limeys had taken Campoleone and slash through to the Alban Hills, while the 3rd Division dogfaces and the Rangers marched into Cisterna to the south.

But the recon force bogged down when it tried to cut across the open ground. The Krauts had a field day, dropping air bursts over them while they tried to drag themselves out of the mud, killing nine men and wounding plenty more. Finally, when darkness fell on January 29, the recon force got the tanks winched back to firm ground, but by then CCA's attack had already begun.

The British drove toward Campoleone, the Scots Guards on one side of the road, the Irish Guards on the other. Both outfits had fought like hell, and they had got exactly nowhere. The air cover system broke down; the planes couldn't get under the low, drizzly clouds, and for some reason, contact between the infantry, artillery and the tanks was always fouling up. First Armored didn't do much fighting—as soon as they tried to attack off the road, they were ass-deep in mud, and from then on it was a salvage opera-

60

tion. The attack on January 30, went nowhere.

There was a rumor that the Rangers had been wiped out down at Cisterna, and that didn't help morale either. Ken Hurley kept thinking, *Whoever made this battle plan must be nuts.*

PFC Hurley rubbed his dripping nose with a mittened hand and scratched the back of his neck where the dark red hair met pink flesh. He felt uncomfortable, but the engines were already turning over, the exhausts spuming in the cold air. Major Tuck's, 1st Battalion was moving out. *Too late now,* he thought. *If I want to go I'll have to use a steel helmet.*

If the damn jerks who had designed these tin cans had ever had to spend a night in one, they'd have had the sense to put in plumbing, he thought morosely. Man, that was the worst part of this war—having to do it in a steel pot and pass it out the pistol port!

Gus Bingham, the driver, put the light tank in gear, and they were rolling down the Albano road, one of a long column. Up beside Ken in the open turret, the tank commander, Sergeant Bammler, kept his field glasses handy. Though what he'd do if they spotted a Panther or a Tiger, Ken didn't know. They sure couldn't fight it, not with a 37 mm. by God!

He remembered Lieutenant Dyer's briefing. Dyer, his young face serious, had said, "Okay, men, here's the word. General Lucas still wants to push a mobile force up the Albano road. The English are going to try for Campoleone again. But Combat Command will try to the northwest—and our outfit, with Force Hightower, will make the main attack along the highway."

Ken could see Colonel Hightower, big-shouldered and thin-haired, issuing his verbal orders from the "Auditorium," his blacked-out deuce-and-a-half. Hightower wore steel spectacles, but he had a thin, fighting mouth—a real soldier, Hightower. No screwing around with him in command.

Dyer had said, "Our mission is to attack through the British 1st Division and seize the heights west of Castel Gandolfo in the Colli Laziali."

"Jeez, that's one of the Pope's palaces," Hurley had blurted.

"Oh? Well, I doubt if he'll be home." Dyer smiled.

There was more poop. Lieutenant Malone of the Recon Company had scouted up the road. He found that the Irish Guards and the Scots Guards had gotten mixed up during the night and fought a hell of a battle with each other. Hooray for the Irish, Ken thought, grinning. But the mixup might foul up the whole effort. Major Huguelet, Hightower's S-3, had gone forward to see what the hell was going on.

But the attack couldn't wait. First Battalion was moving out.

Ken's tank passed a Sherman, an M-4 medium tank, mired in the ditch. The crew of the stuck tank called out as the light tanks passed, "Whatcha gonna do with them sardine cans? The Krauts'll bust you open with pea shooters!" Which wasn't so very far from wrong, as the song went.

61

"Go to hell!" Ken hollered back, flushing to the roots of his red hair. "A bloody 88 can't hurt us any more'n it would that mud plow you're ridin'!" Which was also true. A Tiger, with its 88, or even a Mark IV Panther with its 77, could blast hell out of any tank in the division. Of course, the division mediums could do likewise—if they could get close enough. The only way American armor could fight Kraut tanks effectively was to maneuver with their greater speed and usually greater numbers and hit the heavily armored, big-gunned Kraut vehicles in the sides or ass.

Now there were British soldiers on either side of them, in the ditches. There was shooting all along the road, a loud crackle as of a thousand twigs breaking at once just forward. Some two hundred men of the 2 Foresters were attacking up the road, with a few tanks from the 46 Royal Tank Regiment lumbering beside them, trying to pin down the Krauts.

The major in charge of the Foresters knelt beside Ken's tank, talking with the American officers. "Jerry is heavily fortified in Campoleone Station," he said in his clipped voice. "The ground is heavily mined off the road on both sides, and Jerry's got quite a lot of SP guns and tanks up ahead. We'll try to go in to clean them out for you."

Bully for you, Ken thought. And that was the last time he'ld ever knock the Limey's, bless their black hearts. For the British went forward into the sleet of German fire and steel doggedly, with stolid courage. Up ahead of the light tanks, there were bodies all over the road, and in the ditches. The British kept attacking, but even Ken could see they were going to run out of men a long time before they made the thousand yards or so into Compoleone.

Lieutenant Dyer was signaling for his tanks to leave the road. *Here we go,* Ken thought. With his platoon of five tanks, Dyer cut off to the right of the Albano highway, headed down through the steep ravines. The light American tanks could cross this particular terrain where the heavies of the Royal Tank Regiment couldn't, and 1st Battalion was going to flank into Campoleone Station.

"Put a goddamn round in the chamber," Sergeant Bammler ordered. Ken slammed home a long, slender 37, watched the breech block lock.

"Up!" He tapped the gunner, Gorman, on the leg. Gorman nodded.

Dyer had found a tankable path through the gullies, and across the little muddy stream that crossed in front of them. Now his tank roared up ahead, skirting a high railway embankment. They would have to find a way across that embankment, too.

Whang! Whang! Small-arms fire zinged off the steel hulls of the tanks. There were German snipers along these gullies. Ken knelt low in the tank, pulled the hatch down over him. Bammler did the same; they couldn't see too well through the vision slits, but it was better than a bullet in the chops.

Blam! Crash! No one who had heard that sound would ever forget it. A

62

high-velocity gun, the shriek of splitting metal—*Jeez*, Ken thought. Up ahead, Dyer's tank slued, smoke pouring from the turret and from the jagged hole the 88 had made in its side.

"Christ, Lieutenant, get out!" Ken heard himself scream. When the Krauts zeroed in on you, you had about five seconds before the next round. There was a story in the division that while it was mathematically impossible for all five men to leave a tank at the same instant, witnesses had seen it happen, seen three men come through a hatch which could only pass one man at a time.

But no one evacuated the stricken vehicle. Ken had been told that while an 88 armor-piercing projectile was only a little slug of tungsten steel, once it blasted into a tank it didn't have the velocity to break through both sides, and it bounced around inside, maybe ricocheting a couple of dozen times. He felt sick.

Whup! That was a sound you wouldn't forget either—an 88 passing a few inches over your head. Hearing the tortured air scream, Ken shook uncontrollably. My God, how did he get out of this damn cracker box?

Pow! Gorman had fired at something, not waiting for Bammler's order. A good gunner kept alert; he didn't have to be told, no matter how they did it at Fort Knox. *Scrape-clang!* Choking on cordite fumes, Ken slapped a fresh projectile into the breech. He wished Gorman wasn't so quick on the trigger; one time he had almost lost an arm for Ken, firing before he could get his arm out of the recoil path. *Pow!*

The AT guns along the railway embankment were dug in. Jeez, the Krauts must be laughing at these stupid sardine cans and their little popguns, banging away. *Blam-whuuup! Blam! Blam!*

"Driver! Back back!" Bammler croaked. There wasn't anything else to do; they would get creamed here. The light tanks backed into the safety of a gulley. *Whap-whap-whap!* German artillery kept air bursts blossoming over the buttoned-up tanks, to keep any infantry from coming up to root out the AT gun nests.

But the infantry tried it. In their flattish, soup-bowl helmets, the Foresters ran forward, their long British bayonets jutting from their stubby Enfields. *Brrrp-Brrrp-brrrp!* A couple of Schnauzer MGs, which had lain doggo, waiting for the foot troops, opened up, crisscrossing the fields with flying steel. The British lines melted away. One Tommy, a short lad with a wizened face, crawled back past Ken's tank, crying and dragging a shattered foot in the mud.

Out in front of the tanks another wounded man was screaming crazily. *For God's sake, don't try again!* Ken thought, feeling the words trying to burst from his lips. *Oh, you crazy, beautiful, black British buggers, give it up!*

Brrrrrp-brrrrp-brrrrp! Wow-wow-wow-wow! Mud fled in front of another

British squad, trying to flank the embankment. Its corporal fell on the grenade he had been about to throw, severing his own head. The squad melted into the mud. None of them moved.

A British officer, a single black pip heavy on his battle jacket, was walking between the tanks, crying out something to the men huddled in the gullies. *You silly bastard, get down,* Ken wanted to shout. *Crack—Crack! Whang!* Half the lousy Kraut army must be shooting at him.

"Different concept," Sergeant Bammler was saying crazily, watching the English officer. "Different attitude." Bammler was a college man who could come up with a lot of crazy comments.

The British lieutenant strolled across to the gulley, bobbed down out of sight, Then he lifted up and waved his swagger stick at the tanks. The meaning was plain: *No go, chums. You might as well go back.*

Ken wasn't scared any more; somehow the bowels that had been churning and growling all the way up front were like iron. He wasn't scared now—but he was so mad the tears ran from his eyes. If they could only maneuver! If they could only get off the goddamn roads, swing wide through the fields! Then they'd see who ran, who left their goddamn blood in the mud!

The Pope didn't have to worry, if he was at Castel Gandolfo. No two hundred Britishers and a lousy battalion of light tanks was going to break through Campoleone today. The English were streaming back now, half of them carrying their wounded buddies. A hot shame swept over Ken Hurley. Only one tank had got it—Lieutenant Dyer's. The poor British doughfeet had caught all the hell, while the tanks sat back—but mad as he was, Ken realized that to send the tanks forward, before the AT guns were rooted out, would have merely resulted in the loss of all of them.

He would never bitch about being in the dirty little garbage scows again. Sure, these tin sides wouldn't stop an 88—but the OD shirts of the doughs out there wouldn't stop a thrown rock. The poor bastards!

Colonel Hightower was on the radio, calling off the attack. They were meeting more Krauts along the whole line than anyone had dreamed could be at Anzio. First Armored Division was ordered back, to a blocking position in the woods north of Anzio-Nettuno.

Eight miles back, in the woods, it was hard work for each member of the crew. Tankers rode, while the doughs walked, but there was a price. When you stopped, you had to pull maintenance, grease the tracks, clean off the mud, oil the MGs, swab the bore of the cannon. If it took all night, you had to do it. But Ken Hurley, who had seen the sprawled corpses of the doughs along the Albano road, would never bitch again.

No, sir. It was plenty good just to be alive.

Gorman and Gus Bingham had finished putting the breech block of the 37 mm. back together, while Ken swabbed the machine-gun barrels. On a

64

tank crew, it didn't matter what your job was, you all pitched in. Any man could take any other man's place, if he had to.

There was still plenty of noise from the front, seven-eight miles to the east and north. Flashes, too. But in the woods it was peaceful and—*wheeee-ee-ee-bram! Whooo-oooo-oo-crump-crump! Boom-Boom!* Fire blossomed in the dark woods, thunder rolled. Slowly, steadily, German artillery began to search the beachhead. That was big stuff, which could reach any position in the beachhead area, Ken knew. *Whee-eee-bram!* In the next clump of pine trees, a man cried out, choking.

"Oh, drop one in anywhere, you lousy bastards!" Ken shouted. "You can't miss!"

Sergeant Bammler, in charge of the platoon, came back from Battalion CP. "Seems we'll stay here awhile, fellows. The brass have called off the big attack. Now we've got to dig the tanks in—slit trenches, too."

With a shovel off the tank, Ken threw up a divot of earth. Water spurted out, filled the hole. "Dig in!" he yelled. "We'll be up to our ass in water!"

"Can't help it," Bammler said frowning. "We'll be under fire."

Ken Hurley forgot his resolve never to bitch again. For as he stood arguing with Bammler, it began to rain.

While the British were dying before Campoleone Station, and the 1st Armored Division was floundering in the mud along the Albano road, 3rd Division had been pressing toward Cisterna, the most important hub of the southern part of the beachhead. Two days after the attack jumped off, January 30, it was still trying to take Cisterna.

In the CP of the 3rd at Conca, Major General Lucian K. Truscott limped about on his bad leg. He was a striking figure in his russet leather jacket, shiny helmet and cavalry boots. The dogfaces knew him each time he went up to the front: that was one reason for the spectacular garb. He had discovered another good reason to wear cavalry boots. But for the high, tough leather encasing his leg, the bomb fragment which had struck him down on the twenty-fourth would have seriously injured him.

Now, still croaking hoarsely from the sore throat he had developed in this wet weather, he talked with the corps commander, General Lucas. General Johnny Lucas was not happy.

The American offensive had gotten off to a bad start everywhere, but especially with the loss of the Rangers. Mark Clark had hit the ceiling over that news! Clark was worried over the bad publicity from the Rapido fiasco, and the Ranger loss, unavoidable as it had been, was one more shock for the home front. Truscott was thinking, that was one trouble with Mark Clark. He was a good administrator, no doubt of that, and he went to bat for his subordinates every time—but he could not keep from worrying about bad publicity.

Too, Clark didn't seem able to keep his fingers on the pulse of battle. It was a sort of sixth sense, this ability; some generals had it, some did not. Truscott himself had it. General Harmon, of the 1st Armored, had it, too, as did Iron Mike O'Daniels, Truscott's Deputy Division Commander.

Johnny Lucas, too, had had it once. Now, Truscott thought, Lucas looked tired, and sick.

He asked Lucas what General Alexander had to say about the situation on his last visit to the beachhead.

"Alexander? Oh, he was kind enough," Lucas muttered, taking off his steel-framed GI glasses. "But I'm afraid he is not pleased. My head will probably fall in the basket—but I've done my best. There were just too many Germans here for me to lick." He sighed. "I told Clark yesterday I was sent on a desperate mission, one with the odds greatly against success. Actually, we're better off now than we had any right to expect."

Truscott looked at the operations map of the 3rd Division front, frowning. The map didn't give much encouragement. He knew now he was facing two full divisions instead of the battered Hermann Göring. He turned back to Lucas, his square chin stubborn, his gray hair shining handsomely in the lamplight. Well, he was giving it all he could.

Lucas seemed wrapped in his own thoughts. Poor Johnny! Clark was up to the beachhead day after day, establishing an advance Fifth Army CP, moping around, making Lucas miserable by looking over his shoulder. Of course, Clark was responsible, too, for Lucas' actions—but he made no attempt to take command of the beachhead.

There was no doubt that Clark was unhappy over the lack of progress the last nine days. And Alexander had been openly critical of the slowness with which VI Corps developed its attack. General Devers, who was American Deputy Commander in the Mediterranean, had arrived on the beachhead, too, and he had told Truscott that Lucas looked tired and ill. Well, Lucas was. This war was no picnic for a general.

But if Clark wanted Lucas to go all out, he could order it. But Clark had never changed Lucas' original orders. Perhaps the Rapido affair had shaken Clark, or perhaps he had never really grasped the essence of the Anzio situation. A man had a sense of battles, or he did not.

In Truscott's own book, Lucas had been dead right in not moving inland too soon. Six Corps had no strength, only two divisions at the start, and while they could have undoubtedly reached the Colli Laziali, they would have been cut off. Truscott had never believed that Kesselring would be rattled by the landings. Lucian Truscott was a fighting general, and he always figured the other' side would fight, too.

But if he, Truscott, had been in command, VI Corps would have moved more rapidly, once the beachhead had been secured. Seven days seemed too long, especially since he expected the Germans to send fresh troops. Truscott himself had prodded for permission to take Cisterna some days before the offensive started. They had to have Cisterna to accomplish their mission of cutting the German communications, and now, on the first day of February, it seemed their chances of taking it were growing remoter every hour.

Lucas put his glasses back on, ran a veined hand through his sparse, cropped, white hair, and talked about the Ranger operation.

Clark had thrown a real flap, all right. He was damned upset, and had implied the Rangers weren't capable of handling the kind of mission they had been given. Truscott had told Clark that he himself had helped to organize the force back in '42, and that he and Colonel Darby had a better idea of what the Rangers could do than other American officers. Clark had talked of ordering an investigation to fix responsibility. Truscott told him the responsibility was Truscott's alone, that he considered the mission well within the capabilities of such fine soldiers. Clark dropped the matter.

Now, VI Corps was to send the Rangers back to the States—what was left of them. It was too bad, for their undeserved failure would be held against all other troops of their kind.

Then Lucas mentioned the British front. The Limeys were catching hell, trying to attack. General Penney's 1 Division had lost half their effectiveness, and Lucas was worried. He didn't see how the British were going to break through.

Finally, the talk came to 3rd Division's situation. Truscott briefed Lucas quickly. First Battalion, 7th Infantry, had reached the railway line west of Cisterna, taking more than two hundred prisoners. First Battalion, 30th Infantry, had reached a stream about one mile west of the town. Second Battalion, 15th Infantry, was at the outskirts of Cisterna itself. They had radioed for permission to blast their way into town after dark.

Lucas wanted to know how many men Truscott had lost since D-Day.

"More than three thousand battle casualties. About one-third of my armor."

Lucas winced. There were no more reserves. If the 15th Infantry entered Cisterna, there was no way to reinforce them. He ordered Truscott to hold them back.

Truscott agreed reluctantly; he had already told the battalion commander the same thing.

Lucas mentioned that all they could do was to consolidate the ground that had been taken and try to reorganize. When reinforcements arrived on the beachhead, the attack would be renewed. He said, "I hit Alexander up for two more divisions while he was here. All he gave me was a goddamn enigmatic little smile . . ."

After a bit, Lucas departed. He hated to stop attacking, but there was nothing else to do. After he had gone, Truscott stood looking at his map, feeling that sixth sense of battle in his finger tips. He was thinking, *Keeping the enemy off balance now is a forlorn hope. The initiative is passing to the Germans, and we are about to start fighting for our lives. . .*

While the American offensive inched toward Cisterna and finally stalled, the American commanders could have no idea of the near-desperation of the German defenders. Although American intelligence, felt the two sides were close to equal, with an edge in numbers to the Germans, actually the, Germans were outnumbered in combat troops. But beyond that, the Germans were not fighting as organized divisions. They were a jumble of units, hurriedly thrown into battle, operating under strange headquarters and unknown commanders. Here the advantage lay with the attackers.

Kesselring, who had insisted upon the gamble, thought it a miracle that the German troops held at all. He had been perfectly willing to sacrifice them for time; since, when the OKW—the High Command—had promised to aid him, he knew veteran troops would soon arrive. Even if the enemy forces had reached the Colli Laziali, he would have continued to try to contain them. For when help came, it would come in great strength, to wipe out the beachhead once and for all.

The threat in the German rear was very real. They could not ignore it, not for an instant. The OKW, in all, diverted eight new divisions to the Italian front. They arrived in bits and pieces, fragments. But they arrived, each unit seemingly just in the nick of time.

That the Germans fought well is an understatement. That they were lucky is equally true.

This February 1 they were somewhere in Italy, *Oberleutnant* Christian Strubing knew. More than that, he didn't know, and he didn't much care. *Mein Gott*, how they had been crisscrossed and backtracked, waiting in tunnels, shifting from one rail to another, all the way from southern France! On the damned train it had been impossible to get much sleep, even though as *oberleutnant* commanding Number 3 Company, 715th Infantry Division, he had been entitled to sleeping space.

The weather had been cold and damp—fortunately, though, the clouds kept the Ami Air Force off their backs—and the idiot engineers had kept the whistles shrieking all the way. So they were in a hurry! The war would wait—wars always waited, until you got there.

Oberleutnant Strubing had had plenty of experience, finding that out. In the back of his pay book were the citations from many decorations, beginning with the *Einmarsch* into Austria. *Scheiss*, he thought moodily, always going somewhere, and always in such a *Gottverdammten* hurry!

He was a large bear of a man, with red-gold hair on his chest and great hams for hands. When he had been awarded the Austrian campaign medal, he had been a sergeant. But one of the things the *Führer* had done for Germany was that now a man could rise.

The rail lines from northern Italy had been filled with troop trains pouring south. Perhaps—but the devil with perhapses! Strubing's last box of cigars had been packed away with the Company HQ baggage by mistake, and he was as irritable, as a wounded bear as he slogged along through the mud at the head of his company column.

For they had come to the end of the rails at last, somewhere east of a rail junction called Cisterna. Now, moving westward in the night, Strubing could see the continuous flashing, the low, low lightning, in the distance; he could hear the distant rumble, as of thunder.

Up ahead there was battle, and 715th Division was going in.

Plain doughfeet, the 715th. No fancy Panzers in black berets, not even a grenadier designation. Just infantry. But when the battle got tough, it was plain infantry they called for, Strubing thought. *We do the job, take the ground, not the boys in the black berets, not the* Luftwaffe *in their light blue.* Field green, and steel helmets, and bayonets, that was the stuff!

Behind him in the column a man stumbled, and someone, hidden by the darkness, ventured a loud curse. Strubing grinned. There were new boys back there, and they were scared as hell. They were always scared as hell, going in for the first time, and they wanted to talk, curse, jabber, to relieve the tension. You could tell recruits from veterans. The old men kept their yaps shut.

Scheiss, he didn't blame the new men. He had been scared as hell himself when they marched into Austria. Nobody knew what would happen. Even now he was worried. The odds were always in your favor; it took thousands of bullets to kill one man. But a man's luck ran out sooner or later. There were not many of the old crowd left. Heinz dead in Russia, Kohlmar crippled in Africa, Vogelsang killed in France . . .

Aloud, he snapped, "Lieutenant, get the men to singing." That would take their minds off their troubles.

Lieutenant von Fehrenteil's young face looked scared, too. During his years as a *Fahnrich*, an officer candidate, Fehrenteil had seen no, real action. But he was an aristocrat, and that breed always seemed to get commissions. Strubing, a forester, was the first of his family to become an officer.

"Standing by the lamp post, by the barracks gate . . ."

Quickly, the men picked up the song, a version of *Lili Marlene*. *Lili Marlene!* There was a song, by God! Strange, when that Swedish piece, Anderson, introduced it before the war in Berlin, it had flopped. Sickening, the critics had called it. Well, it was the kind of song no civilian could ever understand, or care for. When you slept under clean sheets with your wife, you could not understand the things that moved a soldier.

But the boys in France had picked that song up, made it their own, and later *Rundfunk Belgrad* had played it each night for the men in the Afrika Korps. It was said even the Tommies and the Amis sang it, too.

They all sang it, because in that song was everything a soldier thought about. Back home, the bands played martial music over the radio, and people thought the boys went out to die thinking of home and the *Führer* and the thousand year Reich. *Scheiss!*

"Halt! Halt! Pass the word!"

The low cries came back along the long column of the regiment. The mud squished as the 715th rifle companies halted.

"Gewehr ab! Order arms!" Strubing barked. *Give the boys a rest; soon they'll need it,* Strubing thought.

"Officers forward!"

Strubing moved ahead along the column. Under a large, dripping pine tree he found his regimental commander. The S.O.1, the Operations Officer, was there, too, with the other officers gathering in.

The lieutenant colonel said, "My God, will you listen to the shooting up there! A bad time, I'm afraid. Our line is holding by a thread—we have been moving units up and down the line, to meet the pressure, and the entire reserve is committed. The enemy is almost in Cisterna. They want us to go in piecemeal on the Cisterna front, just as each company arrives. No time to organize a division front. The guides are meeting us now. Gentlemen, *heil* and good luck!"

Back with his company, Strubing snapped, *"Gewehr auf!"* The carbines slapped, going to the shoulders. "Forward!"

The column slogged on through the night, moving closer to the flashes in the west.

Wheee-eee-ee-bram! Bram-bram! Shells struck in front of the column, falling with high-pitched, nasty shriek American shells always had. They said you couldn't hear them, coming in. *Scheiss! Whoo—ooo-ooo—crump-boom-boom!* That big stuff went completely overhead, a different sound.

Somewhere up front, a man had been hit.

"Stretcher-bearer! Stretcher-bearer!"

"Steel helms on," Strubing ordered. "Forward, march!"

Number 3 Company had faced its first fire. It would not be the last.

As the 715th Division moved into line, and as Generals Lucas and Truscott were conferring in the CP at Conca, the intelligence officers of VI

70

Corps were busy. The POW cages were filling up, and there were hundreds of prisoners to interview.

Third Division was getting chewed up in front of Cisterna, but it was doing some chewing itself. Long columns in gray-green overcoats were filing despondently back into the narrow beachhead, hands clasped behind their heads. The men in these columns looked at the massive piles of Allied equipment on the beaches and sometimes they muttered to each other.

In one of the columns marched a bald, unshaven officer who seemed to be past fifty. The intelligence officers pulled him out of line—up front somebody had fouled up. You were supposed to separate officers and NCOs from the other ranks at once.

The chief interrogator, a young, redheaded captain named Marlow, who had gone to school in Switzerland, was not bothered by the fifty-year old *Rittmeister's* appearance. Although his long, field overcoat was ill-fitting and filthy from lying against the soggy ground, and he hadn't shaved in days, Marlow had never seen any of the movie version of Kraut officer-monocled, immaculate, arrogant—out here. Front line officers, of any army, are never very glamorous in appearance.

The *Rittmeister* carried only a little plastic box of butter, a piece of black bread wrapped in muslin, and a can of Norwegian herring. He had also a straight razor and a tiny pair of Solingen steel scissors.

Marlow took the razor from him, explaining that he would be issued a new one after he had left the beachhead. Then Marlow, with his assistant, a Bavarian-born sergeant, asked the questions. They didn't get a hell of a lot, at first.

The prisoner was Edwin Albrecht Wentz, *Rittmeister*, and he was fifty years old. He would not divulge his unit, but they knew that, anyway.

Only when they asked him how he thought the war was going did he speak at any length. He seemed to grow tired, and said, "There is a saying in our army, that it is only the quantities of equipment you have that defeats us. *Die Menge tut's*. We know your air force is dominant, and your artillery is superb. We have a certain myth that your infantry is very poor. But I have seen your Rangers and your 3rd Division fight, and this do not believe. I think, someday, our generals will find this to be true, also. You Americans lack only experience."

Then he said, "I think He has led us into disaster."

Low-voiced, Marlow asked his Bavarian NCO, "What does he mean, He?"

"He means Adolf, sir. These officers never say *der Führer.*"

"*Ja*," Edwin Wentz repeated, not caring who overheard him, "He has led us to disaster."

At Fifth Army CP, there was growing concern in the G-2 Section.

"Cripes," an assistant G-2 officer said, running his hand tiredly over his close-cut brown hair, "we're identifying a hell of a lot of German units!"

Colonel Howard agreed. What he had predicted so stubbornly seemed to be happening. The Germans were reacting vigorously. Intelligence report after report filtered back from the Anzio front, and a frightening total of German units had been positively identified.

The assistant G-2, a captain, read aloud, "Hermann Göring Panzer Division, 26th Panzer, 16th SS. All positive. And now, 65th, 362nd, 1st Parachute, 71st, and 3rd Panzer Grenadier Divisions. Plus the 715th Infantry—cripes, Colonel, that one's supposed to be in France!"

The officers around the G-2 map looked at each other. One said, "Those can't all be full divisions—"

Colonel Howard didn't think they were. His own guess was that Kesselring was sending in small units from many divisions, a battalion here, a regiment there. But could he justify reporting such a guess to General Clark?

They were all thinking the same thing, but no one spoke.

Finally, Colonel Howard headed for the door. The commanding general, Mark Clark, had to be informed. This was going to make Brigadier Strong and himself wonderful prophets—but there was an old saw about prophets.

After he had gone, the junior officers kept looking at the enemy symbols in red on the big map. The terrain surrounding the beachhead bristled with red squares, each with a divisional symbol. "To hell with being right," the brown-haired captain said finally. "I'm thinking about those poor bastards on the beach."

Some hours later, a knot of officers stepped back respectfully as Field Marshall Albert Kesselring approached his own operations map. In German Army Group "C"HQ, confidence was running strong.

The big-nosed, strong-faced General Westphal told Kesselring the Allied attack at Anzio had ground to a halt. Suddenly, everywhere, the enemy had gone on the defensive.

"I wonder if they'll ever know how close they came," Kesselring muttered. His normally pleasant face seemed very tired. "Even after the Allied commander delayed, we were thin—dreadfully thin. Provisional battalions, ragtag units, parts of divisions, all under HQs which had never fought such troops before. The Allies were a cohesive force. If only they had made a greater effort, with more troops . . ."

The German officers did not contradict their commander, but they were thinking part of the miracle lay in the thousand of German corpses in the mud surrounding Anzio. And the fact that Allied air was hamstrung by the weather, and Allied armor could not roll. But that belonged to the past. The future lay in the hands of the German

High Command in Italy.

Westphal said, "Von Mackensen has his orders. Fourteenth Army attacks to split the beachhead, drive the *Allierte* into the sea. Three *Kampfgruppe*, here here and there. When von Mackensen has probed a weak spot . . ." Westphal shrugged. The iron fist would fall, backed by all the power of the *Wehrmacht*. The Beachhead would be erased.

Lance the abscess south of Rome! "He," had ordered it. The scalpel was poised and ready.

7

Stand or Die

"There was a job to be done, and I was a soldier."—Major General Lucian King Truscott, writing of events at Anzio, February 17, 1944

Shortly after midnight, February 3, 1944, U.S. VI Corps went completely over to the defensive. Fifth Army HQ, believing the enemy was in far greater strength than anyone had expected, and that he was prepared to launch a counteroffensive to drive the beachhead into the sea, ordered General Lucas to halt all attacks, dig in, and to hold the Corps Beachhead Line at all costs.

Almost immediately, the German probes began. On February 3, German attacks pinched off all ground gained by the British 1 Division near Campoleone, and on February 4 heavy losses were inflicted on the British once again. The Allied lines buckled backward.

Then, on February 5 a heavy German blow fell against the U.S. 3rd Division.

Harry Bonsal, Platoon Sergeant, 2nd Battalion, 7th Infantry, could look out over his sector of the 3rd Division front and realize it was going to be the very devil to hold. Not that Harry Bonsai knew much about tactics; until the draft caught him in 1941, he had been an insurance adjuster. A shorter than average dark-haired chunky man of twenty-seven he had thought adjusting, with its odd hours and the screwballs you had to do business with a tough job. Like the saying went, he didn't know what tough was!

Not until he got in the 7th Infantry, that is. But he had a good mind, not easily rattled, and he knew how to take orders and carry them out, and he could handle men, if he had to. It hadn't taken him too long to get stripes.

But looking out over his line, he wished someone else had the platoon right now. The position stretched across flat, open fields. It had almost none of the defensive terrain features an infantryman could hope to organize behind. Glumly, Harry figured that if the Krauts meant business, they weren't going to hold long.

He hoped Major Elterich, his battalion commander, or Colonel Sherman, the regimental CO, could get that little point across to General Truscott.

One thing they had done which seemed good was to organize the position in depth. Each of the regiments of the 3rd Division had developed three successive lines of defense, with the last one being the final Corps Beachhead Line. With each regiment spread out in depth, a German penetration ought to be checked more easily. Harry Bonsal liked the idea, even though his own outfit was on the front line. It was comforting to look back and see you had someplace to go.

But as Harry Bonsal and General Truscott were to discover, the plan wasn't worth a damn.

It was just after dark, February 5, when the German concentrations roared in. Artillery, mortar, direct tank fire—the works. Bonsal's men huddled in their water-filled holes, keeping their heads down. God, what a pasting! And Harry knew the Krauts didn't waste ammo just for the hell of it. He was getting softened up for an attack, right in his sector.

And each time he looked up, seeing nothing in front of him but the bare fields stretching into darkness, over which the Krauts would come any minute, he felt himself getting soft, all right. Right in the knees.

Whatever happened, it was up to him. He didn't have a platoon leader; the lieutenant had been hit two days before, and there weren't any spares just yet.

Kingsley, his runner, huddled close to him. "What's gonna happen, Sarge?"

"Quiet!" Harry snapped. "I think I hear tank engines."

Wrroom-wrroom-wrroom! Hell, yes, those were tank engines. They sounded just like airplanes, in the distance. And over there in the east, where the sound came from, there was nothing but Krauts.

"Oh, Jeez, them motors sound awful," Kingsley said. "They don't sound like our tanks at all."

Pop! Pop! Pop; Flares! In the ghastly yellow light, Kingsley's face looked drawn, ghostly. With a start, Harry realized the artillery had stopped falling.

75

But there was no slackening in the noise. *Brrrrp! Brrrrp!* Machine pistols were clattering a hundred yards in front, sending orange-purple winks of light through the wavering darkness.

And somebody was banging on a washtub, it sounded like. It was enough to scare the hell out of you, make you pull your chin in.

Suddenly Harry realized that was what the Krauts were trying to do, scare hell out of the platoon. He got up on his knees, sluing the cold barrel of his heavy M-I around to face the front.

"My platoon!" he shouted. "Heads up! Here they come!"

A long line of lean, ghostly figures in big helmets was running out of the circle of darkness. "Shoot! Shoot!" Harry bawled. He let fly with his own M-1. *Pow! Pow! Pow!*

A grenade sailed through the flickering, wavering light cast by the parachute flares, exploded whitely in his face. He was blinded, but he continued to shoot. *Pow! Pow!* He could hear the Krauts yelling now, as they ran forward. All he could see was expanding red, white and yellow rings in front of his eyes.

As platoon commander, Harry knew, he wasn't supposed to be shooting— he should be directing the fire of his platoon. But somebody had to start it off—*wrang!* the empty clip ejected from his M-1; the rifle was empty.

But now the M-1s and machine guns were cracking all along the line of shallow holes. Blinking his eyes, Harry thought, *Got to get on the wire, call for artillery support.* He fumbled for the field phone lying on the wet earth beside him. Everywhere the infantry went, they slung wire. That was the only way you could get help, or let higher HQ know.

The wire was out.

And at his feet Kingsley was dead, shot through the throat.

Crash! Crash! Crash! A line of fire and singing steel splashed across his front, hardly a hundred yards away. Company HQ was on the ball, directing fire, trying to keep the Krauts off the backs of the outpost platoons. And suddenly the Krauts were gone, as the flares fizzled and went out. Somewhere near him, Harry heard a man crying out brokenly. It didn't sound like an American.

He thought, *Thank the Lord for our artillery. Best damn artillery in the world, 3rd Division's!* General Truscott had those boys trained! The first German assault was broken.

Quickly, he crawled along the line of holes, seeing who was hit, what gaps needed plugging. His nervousness was gone now, in the heat of action. He had things to do. He said to one of the men, "Joe, check the wire."

The Krauts were gone, but they would be back.

At ten o'clock Colonel Carleton, the Division Chief of Staff, was on the party line, talking to Bonsal's regimental and battalion commander. The assault had all the earmarks of the all-out attack VI Corps was awaiting, and Division HQ was tense.

Major Elterich said he was getting the hell kicked out of him, and asked permission to withdraw.

Carleton asked General Truscott to get on the phone.

Elterich told Truscott his 2nd Battalion had suffered heavily, and he could not hold out much longer. Any minute he might be cut off. He asked Truscott to permit him to withdraw to the intermediate line to his rear, on which the 7th Infantry's 3rd Battalion was assembling. Truscott took him at his word, told the battalion to fall back.

But when 2nd Battalion withdrew, its flank battalion from the 30th Infantry had to withdraw, too. On a front of four miles, 3rd Division was back on its intermediate defense line, and just in front of its last-ditch positions.

And the battle for Anzio beachhead was only a few hours old.

The last man of Harry Bonsal's decimated platoon filed into the prepared holes of the intermediate defense line, while Harry checked him off. They had come back in orderly fashion, bringing their dead and wounded. Harry was thinking, *there's plenty of fight in them yet, but there's no sense in getting cut off in exposed positions, when you have a good line prepared behind you.*

He was seeing to it that the platoon was resupplied with ammo when the new orders hit him.

"What do you mean, go back?" he shouted at the runner.

"Orders from Division, Sergeant. Counterattack at once to take back our first defense line!"

His company commander materialized out of the dark.

"That you, Bonsal? Get ready to move out. We're going back!"

"Somebody is slap, screaming nuts!" Harry, said, when the captain had moved on. But he knew better than to show that attitude to the platoon—not if he expected them to follow him.

"Look, boys," he said, when the outraged protests at his announcement had dwindled, "it's like this. The Germans are probing us, trying to smell out a weak spot. If they think we're patsies, later on we'll really catch it. We're going to show them the 7th Infantry can't be pushed around."

Later, he was to learn he was nearer the truth than he had known.

As soon as both the 7th and 30th Regiments co-ordinated, the counterattack jumped off. First, the sharp, slamming, artillery softening up, then up out of the holes, advancing in the dark, bayonets at the ready.

In front of Harry Bonsal, purple-orange flames winked. He heard the nasty passage of slugs close to his head. But in the dark, he did not give the order to fire until they reached the old line. Then, lungs filled for yelling, his platoon were in among the surprised Germans.

A Kraut fired at Harry from a distance of three paces, blinding him. God-damn, he was always getting blinded at the wrong time! Then the Kraut hit him low, knocking him down. Harry saw the dull gleam of a trench knife in the big Kraut's first. With a small scream, he grabbed at the Kraut's arm, try-ing to hold it back. For several seconds they struggled, arm against arm, thrashing and grunting.

Harry couldn't remember any of the holds he had been taught, any of the hand-to-hand combat they had shown him in basic training. All he could do was hang on to that knife arm, rolling in the slippery mud.

He rolled across his own rifle, which he had dropped when the Kraut leaped at him, the bolt grinding into his back. Then the big Kraut pulled his knife hand free, raised it.

Harry hit him in the face with all his strength. The knife came for-ward, ripping along Harry's shoulder. It felt like someone had spilled hot soup on him.

Then the Kraut's eyes bugged out, and he made a couple of gasping nois-es. Kovalics, one of Harry's squad leaders, had bayoneted him from behind. The Kraut fell, silently. Men don't scream when cold steel strikes them; they are often too shocked to cry out.

"You okay, Sarge?"

"Okay, okay," Harry gasped. *Oh, hell, he was going to vomit.* He threw up and, somehow, at once he felt better. He saw dark forms standing about in the night, and barked, "Kovalics! Arthur! Get the men spread out, in holes! What the hell you standing around for? Don't bunch up!"

The Krauts had pulled back when Harry's platoon had entered the old position. It had been easier than anyone expected.

Only when he had found his rifle, cleaned it, and made sure his men were properly spread out did he remember he hadn't even told Kovalics thanks.

Up at Division, General Truscott realized what was wrong, almost as soon as he had authorized the 7th Infantry to withdraw. His defense plan had a fundamental weakness. He had been lucky the Germans hadn't been pre-pared to exploit it.

With three defense lines, the American troops were too thinly spread. Worst of all, the psychology was all wrong. Unconsciously, each man and officer thought of the third and last line as the place where the real stand would be made. They were in no frame of mind to hold the intermediate lines to the end.

So Truscott gave swift orders. Take back the first line, and hold it. It would become the main line of resistance, with two battalions on line, one in reserve in each regiment, and to hell with depth. If the Germans broke into the beachhead, their goose was cooked anyway. Bring the 7th Infantry, the worst battered of the regiments, back to the final line with the Division Engineer Battalion, as Division Reserve.

Throw up wire, put out mines. Move the tanks and tank destroyers up with the infantry—not the school solution for the employment of armor, but Lucian Truscott never much cared for school solutions—to calm the troops' gnawing concern with enemy Panzers.

And the artillery—the key to the defense was the seven battalions of Division Artillery. Truscott had no peer at employment of field artillery. In his division, anyone could call for fire support, forward observers, liaison officers, infantry commanders at any echelon. But commo had a way of going out, so concentrations were planned for every possible avenue of enemy approach, every assembly area, every spot where a Kraut might go. These concentrations were to be fired on call, but if commo went, or observers killed, specified concentrations were to be fired repeatedly until new communications were established:

With this system, the slightest German activity along the front brought down a screaming mass of fire. Now the German probes ran into a brick wall of fire and steel. There would be no more retreat.

And with the dawn, February 6, the last positions of the initial line were completely restored, and Harry Bonsal's platoon went back into reserve. Harry Bonsal had lost one-fourth his effectives, but he had learned a profound lesson in the art of war, one he would never forget.

Sergeant Bonsal was not the only one who had learned a lesson. Eberhard von Mackensen had learned that the 3rd Division front was not the place to make his big push to split the beachhead.

When the might of the *Wehrmacht* fell, it would fall elsewhere. From the 3rd Division, the Germans knew, they would get only bloody noses.

Ten days passed slowly, while both sides continued to build up strength. The initiative remained with the Germans, and they continued to whittle away at the beachhead through limited attacks. Most of these attacks fell in the British zone.

There was nothing the British could do to prevent being pushed back slowly. They lost company position after position, and usually the company with the ground. The 1 Division was under strength, and there were no British replacements in the theater. No troops ever fought with more gallantry, against greater odds. Their losses grew and grew, until the total was staggering.

General Lucas was gravely concerned about the British situation. Unfortunately, Lucas had little confidence in the British; he had never understood or admired their way of doing business. In all fairness, it must be said the British commanders felt the same toward him.

The Anzio beachhead deteriorated slowly, while an uneasy lull settled over most of the front lines. After repeated requests from Lucas, the theater sent a new British division, the 56th, to relieve the battered 1st. The relief was completed on February 16, and the 1 Division passed into reserve.

General Lucas, tired and worn, wrote in his diary: "Things get worse and worse." He knew that "top side was not completely satisfied with his work." He was right. Back at Allied Force HQ, General Alexander was saying that he thought Lucas was tired and defeated, and he and Lieutenant General Jacob L. Devers, the American Deputy Theater Commander, began to put pressure on Mark Clark to do something about the Anzio situation.

Then, on February 16, the whole perimeter blazed with German fire. Unmanned tanks, called Goliaths, filled with explosives, crashed into the Allied lines, blowing up wire and fortifications. Observers reported large formations of German troops moving in column toward the beachhead.

It soon became apparent that the heaviest fire was falling in the zone of the 45th Division, which had taken up positions along the Albano road south of Carroceto. At VI Corps HQ, the air was electric with tension. General Lucas and his chief officers showed a certain amount of anxiety.

There were attacks and probes in the 3rd Division zone, in front of Cisterna. The massive artillery fires of the 3rd beat these off easily, and a German battalion was annihilated. In the early night of February 16, General Truscott turned in early. He expected a busy day on the morrow.

His rest was to be short.

In the first minutes of February 17, Colonel Carleton burst into General Truscott's sleeping quarters at Conca. "Boss, I hate to do this, but you'd give me hell if I held this until morning." He banded Truscott a message form. It was a message from Mark Clark to VI Corps:

ORDERS ISSUED THIS DATE AS FOLLOWS X MAJOR GENERAL TRUSCOTT RELIEVED FROM COMMAND OF THIRD DIVISION AND ASSIGNED AS DEPUTY COMMANDER SIXTH CORPS X BRIGADIER O'DANIELS TO COMMAND THIRD DIVISION X COLONEL DARBY TRANSFERRED FROM RANGER FORCE TO THIRD DIVISION X ALL ASSIGNMENTS TO TAKE EFFECT SEVEN-TEEN FEBRUARY. . . .

No one had so much as mentioned this change to Truscott, and he was mad as hell. He had the feeling he was being used to pull someone else's chestnuts out of the fire. And he had the very human desire to remain with his beloved 3rd Division, one of the proudest outfits in the Army.

It was not that he objected to serving under General Lucas; they were old friends, and Lucas had been more than considerate with him in their dealings. But Truscott was not blind to the fact that Lucas was not inspiring confidence in either the High Command or the troops, and that the British wanted him removed. Truscott and Lucas had different methods of command, and Truscott had no desire whatever to leave a post where he had both responsibility and command authority for one in which he would have neither. It was one hell of a situation to place him in, he thought.

But Truscott was a soldier, and obviously there was a job to be done. He could only carry out the order loyally.

When Lucas got the message, he said, "I think this means my relief and that he gets the corps. I hope I am not to be relieved from command. I knew when I came here I was jeopardizing my career because I knew the Germans would not fold up because of two divisions landing on their flank."

In the early morning hours, Truscott called a conference with General O'Daniels, Colonel Darby and his regimental commanders. A division' commander cannot just walk out of his command; there were details to be settled. While the talks were proceeding, Lieutenant Colonel Yarborough, commanding the attached 504th Parachute Battalion, called from his position on the extreme left of the division sector next to the 45th zone. From his command post roof Yarborough could see thousands of Germans advancing into the 45th area. He was directing repeated fire missions by the division artillery.

Just past noon, when Truscott had sent his aide, Captain Bartash, to reopen his trailer back beside Corps HQ on the beach at Nettuno, General Keiser, Corps Chief of Staff, phoned. He wanted to know when Truscott would report.

Colonel Carleton told Keiser the general was on his way.

General Keiser said, "Well, he'd better hurry, because I don't know whether there'll be any Corps HQ by tomorrow morning. We'll probably all be driven into the sea!"

Truscott found a feeling of hopelessness, almost desperation, when he reported into Corps HQ. There was extremely heavy fighting in the British and 45th zones on both sides of the Albano road. The situation, in fact, was far graver than anyone in the 3rd Division had realized.

The 179th Infantry, 45th Division, had suffered heavily, and had been driven back to the final line. The 180th, under extreme pressure, was falling back. German tanks had passed the Corps Beachhead Line, at least two being destroyed in the American positions. South of Carroceto, the 157th Infantry was holding on under heavy attack and begging for help.

General Lucas ordered General Eagles, CG of the 45th to commit his reserve to restore his battle position, and he ordered General Harmon, CG of the 6th Armored, to send a battalion to relieve pressure on the 179th.

Then commo went bad, and no report was received from Eagles, Harmon or the British commander, General Templar. Lucas was desperate.

Truscott, talking with Colonel Langevin, the Corps G-2, and Hill, the G-

3, was optimistic. He said nothing ever looked so bad on the ground as it did on a map at HQ. His statement did nothing to dispel the gloom.

Then Truscott set off from the HQ for the front, to see what he could learn.

He found Generals Harmon and Eagles in good spirits. The situation was serious, but neither general was panicky. Harmon's tank attack had not regained any lost ground, but it had halted the German tanks. Eagles had no communications with his front line battalions, but he remained confident that the 45th Division would hold, and he had ordered a counterattack at dawn. There was nothing more Truscott could do, except to instill optimism with his own fighting spirit. After dark on the seventeenth he returned to Nettuno.

That night General Lucas called a conference of commanders, but no solution to the danger was reached. The beachhead could only continue to fight for its life. At midnight, the conference broke up.

By morning, the Germans had driven a salient four miles deep into the center of the American lines along the Albano road, and six German divisions had been identified within this salient. One battalion of the 45th had been completely cut off south of Carroceto and, generally, there was no communication with the front line battalions.

General Eagles had one battalion in reserve, and General Harmon had his 6th Armored Infantry and tanks. A brigade of the British 56 Division was due to unload at Anzio that morning. As far as Truscott was concerned, the beachhead still had assets.

The officers at VI Corps talked about what to do. Truscott called for a counterattack.

While the argument went on, General Clark flew in from Caserta. He asked Lucas, "What do you propose to do?"

Truscott answered for the corps commander. "I think we should counterattack with everything we have!"

"What have you got to counterattack with?"

Truscott told him of Harmon's tanks and the British brigade, and of the 3rd Division's Infantry, which was uncommitted.

"How soon could you organize this attack?"

"By tomorrow morning, General."

Clark went to the map, touched the shoulders of the German salient with his fingertips. He said, "You should hold these shoulders firmly, and then counteratack against the flanks of the salient."

Until Clark arrived, Lucas opposed the counterattack, for he feared to commit his Corps Reserve. Now that Clark had spoken, Lucas reluctantly agreed. He appeared horribly tired and worried.

Quickly, the details were arranged It was a simple plan, but the best battle plans are always simple. Harmon would form Force H, with the 6th

Armored Infantry and tanks, and the 30th Infantry Regiment. Force H would attack on a converging axis with Force T, the new British brigade under Templar. The attacks would be supported by all the artillery fires the corps could muster, and Clark would call for a maximum air effort in support. By noon, February 17, the details were complete and orders issued.

Then Clark asked Truscott to accompany him up to General Eagles' CP. Clark wanted to talk with Truscott privately. The got into Truscott's jeep, driven by Sergeant Barna.

On the way, Clark said, "You will probably replace Lucas in command within the next four or five days, just as soon as this crisis has passed."

"I have no desire to relieve Lucas," Truscott told him. "Johnny is a personal friend. I didn't want this assignment to Corps. I took it without protest only because I realize that some of the command, especially on the British side, have lost confidence in Lucas. I think we can overcome our difficulties, and I am perfectly willing to continue on as Lucas' deputy as long as necessary."

"I appreciate that," Clark replied. "I do not want to hurt Johnny Lucas either. At any rate, there'll be no change for the present."

Harmon was ordered to attack with Force H anyway. The attack was delayed until 0630, February 19.

Early the next morning, before leaving for his own CP at Caserta, Clark came into Corps HQ and approved the attack plans. There was one change—mines dropped by German planes on Anzio had delayed the landing of the British 169 Brigade. Force T would not be ready.

The situation was still grave. It was agreed at Corps that all commanders would go among front line units, making certain every man understood that he must not give up another foot of ground. Six Corps was back to a line that had nothing behind it but the beaches and the sea.

The point was easy to get across. Almost every soldier could look over his shoulder and see the blue. Tyrrhenian Sea shining at his back.

It was stand or die.

Hermann Gauss, *Gefreiter, Infanterie Lehr Regiment,* shivered with cold, for the day was gloomy, overcast—*nein,* that was excitement, not cold. For the highly regarded Infantry Lehr was going in. Infantry Lehr would be the final blow that would split the Allied beachhead like a rotten apple, so that it's two halves could be chewed up at leisure by von Mackensen's Fourteenth German Army.

Gauss, a big, lean peasant boy from Pomerania, with a short nose and ruddy, square face under his steel helm, had been well briefed by his officers. They had told him how the Allies had inferior numbers, and how they were reeling from the terrible blows of the *Wehrmacht.* And their morale—*ach,* they knew Churchill and Roosevelt had abandoned them to die on this miserable beachhead, and they were ready to surrender.

Ja, it would be easy. This he knew, because his officers had told him. This February 18, with five German regiments, including Infantry Lehr, attacking the shattered 45th Division with many tanks—this would be *der Tag!*

He said to Mayer, his marching companion in ranks, as they marched toward the sound of gunfire, "A good day. The overcast will prevent Allied air from strafing us." Ami infantry wasn't much, but even German soldiers not be expected to fight without air cover.

The regiment was in the approach march, moving through the muddy, broken country along the Albano road.

"*Achtung! Enemy aircraft!*"

With every man in the column, Gauss and Mayer swung heads. It was only a little liaison plane, they saw, like the ones German generals used to fly over the front. They carried no guns or bombs.

Crack! Crrrack! Whap!

"Air bursts!" Mayer screamed. There was no more terrifying sound in the world, When you were in the open. Too late, Gauss remembered the little planes spotted for the artillery. "*Deckung!* Hit the ground!"

The air bursts cracked like thunder, sending black trails of smoke spuming overhead. Beside Gauss a man cried out.

Gauss lifted his rifle and fired at the little plane. All along the road men did the same, and the small, buzzing plane veered away.

"On your feet! On your feet! Forward!"

Now the regiment moved forward at the run. Along the, road it left many of its numbers. It was Gauss' first encounter with the *schreckliche* Ami artillery. That artillery was doing much to tear the German assault to shreds before it could get started.

"Fix bayonets!"

Gritting his teeth, Gauss ran forward, as his platoon. spread out in a thin line. Not for nothing did he hold the infantry assault badge!

There—there were the Panzers, the Tigers and Panthers. They laid down a withering fire for the infantry to advance behind.

It was late in the afternoon, and this was the final push, to end the battle.

But, *Herr Gott!* the ground was littered with broken bodies in field green, and scattered German equipment lay all about in front of the Ami positions. That was the Ami 180th Infantry up there, which Gauss had heard was composed of Red Indians from Oklahoma. They were still holding.

The lighter Ami tanks were not trying to duel with the superior Tigers— but they moved back along the roads, seeking German infantry, breaking it up. But there was no time to worry about that now. Ahead, across a brush-lined creek, Gauss could see the Ami positions.

Forward! It cost men, good German blood, this hot rush of men against men, but Gauss understood an omelet is not made without breaking eggs. *Forward! Hurrah, and hurrah!*

Yelling, Infantry Lehr attacked.

"Christ's sake, here they come!" George Held shouted.

A private first class, he was his squad's BAR man. Next to him, his buddy Joe Alexander handed him a fresh magazine while he shifted his feet in the icy water of their two-man foxhole. Joe's thin face was white. All day they had held this forward position, while the platoon and the company had melted around them. They hadn't had any orders for three hours. For all they knew, the lieutenant was dead. That was the only way you could get out of here—die or go nuts. At Anzio, nobody ever got taken off line, not ever.

And with those yelling Kraut bastards coming down the draw, it was too late to go nuts now, George Held thought. He swung the Browning automatic rifle to cover the onrushing platoon, feeling the sharp bite of fear.

Having spent most of his life in the open, on the range, George had a good eye for distances. He squinted a brown eye, set the battle sight. His leathery face was grim.

Jesus, would the bastards never quit coming?

Brrap-brap-brap-brap-brap-brap!

He let go a long burst, saw a German sprawl in the mud. They were shooting at him and Joe, but everyone knew the dirty Nazis couldn't hit the side of a barn with a rifle. Couldn't shoot like the Oklahoma ranchers in this platoon anyway. Otherwise, somebody'd have picked him and Joe off before now.

Brrrrp! He heard the machine pistol slugs spatter behind him. Long-range—but those damn machine pistols scared the hell out of him. You didn't have to know how to aim with one of those!

Brap-rap-rap-rap-blam! Oh, Christ, why the hell hadn't he taken that agricultural deferment, like the men on the board said he could have? His dad had begged him, too.

Hell, it was no disgrace to raise beef—the Army needed beef. George screwed his round, creased face into a knot.

But the Army needed men, too. And here he was, like a damn fool!

Joe cried out, "ohh!" He grasped at his shoulder and slumped against the side of the hole.

George Held reached for Joe, but it was already too late. The rifle slug had torn out his shoulder blade. He was almost dead.

Shaking with fear and rage, George swung the BAR again. He saw three, four, five Krauts fall, before the BAR clicked dry. He dropped the rifle, scrabbled for a grenade. He got three in the air before they were on top of him. Then he ducked deep into the hole.

Bam! Bam! Bam!

A wounded Kraut fell into his hole, blood running down his sharp-nosed face. Screaming, George put his bayonet into the man with his left hand. The Kraut flopped about, with the bayonet sticking into his gut, trying to get out of the hole. Then he died, and slumped down, his face going under the two feet of muddy water at the bottom.

George had the BAR loaded again. He swung it, but there was nothing to shoot at. The Germans were gone.

In front of his foxhole, a wounded Kraut moved feebly, his blue eyes sickly intent on George. Held knew the Kraut expected to be shot.

He put the muzzle of the BAR on the Kraut. The man closed his eyes, saying something in German. His ruddy, square face twitched.

"Hell!" George said. He didn't want to pull the trigger. He didn't know what to do. Joe was dead. It was ten-fifteen yards to the next hole, and he didn't know who was still around. He was in no shape to take prisoners.

He took his feet out of the dirty water at the bottom of his hole, shook them. *Ouch!* He knew what they looked like—the thought made him sick. Black, swollen—trench foot! If he took his shoes off, he'd never get them back on again. He remembered you didn't get a Purple Heart for trench foot—or was it frostbite? He couldn't remember. He wondered if they had to cut your feet off.

He looked back at the Kraut, who still had his eyes shut. "Oh, crap, I won't kill you, buster," he said, his voice shaking a little. There were too many damned corpses around here already. He refused to look at Joe.

Two hours later, after dark, the medics came up and took Joe away. They also took the wounded Kraut. George Held lay back in his stinking hole, trying to rest.

Maybe the Krauts would attack again—maybe they wouldn't. At any rate the 180th Infantry had held.

At 0630, February 19, Force Harmon, which had been designated to make the great counterthrust, was ready to jump off. Force Harmon had marched eight miles along the German flank, and it was going to punch into the German salient near Carroceto. But there were complications.

Once again the Germans were attacking down the Albano road, and the 45th Division was staggering. Six Corps wanted Harmon to go back, reinforce the danger point along the road. But General Harmon, like Truscott, had the sense of battle in his fingertips. Harmon argued with Corps, getting them to agree that a counterattack into the Krauts' flank would do more good than to take up blocking positions.

If it didn't, Lieutenant Wallace Dewey knew, the beachhead was doomed.

Dewey was a tall, angular man, the kind who had to hunch down in a tank turret. It was hard for him to recall now, after two years of war, that he had taught high school three years before. He didn't wear his glasses much any more; his eyes weren't so bad after all, and it was his one vanity.

Somehow, the men of the 1st Armored weren't the kind a typical, stooped-over, four-eyed, thirty-five-year-old schoolmaster should be leading.

But there was nothing wrong with Wallace Dewey's brain or body, if you forgot his appearance. He was as tough as they came, and in North Africa he had proved it.

"Turn 'em over," he said, and he heard the roar as the engines of his medium tank company came to life. God, it was a fine sound!

Standing tall in the turrret, he heard voices crackle in his earphones. He acknowledged the order, then said over his company net, while his loader operated the radio, "Move out!"

Task Force Harmon was on the road. Ahead, there were nothing but Krauts, and the fate of Anzio beachhead.

There were good roads along here; they had chosen the place for the counterthrust well. Little feeder roads, built by Mussolini to show the wonders of Fascism to a doubting world, but with good hard, surfaces. In building these roads, Wallace thought, Mussolini was helping to end his own system—but how could anyone have known that, ten years back?

Ahead of Force Harmon roared all the massed fires of the Anzio beachhead—artillery, naval gunfire, air support. The artillery was now very effective indeed, for General Truscott had organized all corps artillery along the lines he used in the 3rd Division.

The German lines rocked and flamed—and Force Harmon burst through. For two hours it was easy. Dewey realized they had caught the Germans by surprise, turned their flank.

In front of his tanks streamed a German convoy of trucks and foot troops. "Fire!" he said, completing the fire command, and his own tank gun joined the chorus. His entire company was firing while on the move. God, a fine sight!

Blam! Blam! Blam! German trucks were burning, German infantry were running in all directions. But not all of them. Some of them lay face down in the road.

Now enemy tanks clanked toward them. Over there, desperate Kraut officers had called for help. The Armored opened up a blistering fire with AP shells. A German Mark IV stopped, smoking—and then the ammo in its turret blew.

Beautiful! Beautiful! Wallace Dewey breathed. *There must be some part of me that loves destruction. But it is only the destruction of an evil system, only that.* He had no joy in the thought that in that flaming coffin German tankers had roasted alive.

The guns of Force Harmon were concentrated, its armor a shining spearhead that struck into the German rear and flank with stunning force. It could not be blunted.

Leaving the burning hulks of many German tanks behind them, Force Harmon rolled on. Saving the big stuff now, Dewey's tankers turned their machine guns on the fleeing German infantry. Some ran into farmhouses along the roads, and when they did this, the tanks threw a 75 or two into the houses after them.

By afternoon Force Harmon had shot up thousands of demoralized German infantrymen. But now it was stabbing into the heart of the German Fourteenth Army, and its flow was slowing. On all sides, resistance increased. The Germans were fighting back savagely, as they always did.

Wallace Dewey thought of the armored hoplite of ancient Nineveh, standing in the breach of his city's walls, fighting savagely for the perpetuation of his brutal, militaristic system. Those ancient Assyrians had been dead, when the massed forces of their former slaves had reached their walls, but they had not realized it. They had fought on, until they were so obliterated only their name survived. So *let it be with the Nazis.* Like the Assyrian, they had come down like the wolf on the fold, and like the Assyrian tyrant, they had found the sheep could have teeth. And like the Assyrian, they would be destroyed.

At 1620, its massed guns hot from firing, Force Harmon stopped. General Harmon had reached his objective, halfway to Carroceto. To go further would be foolhardy, even though the enemy was exhausted, ready to break off his offensive against the beleagured beachhead.

But the tide of battle had turned. Aggressive, vigorous action, as General Truscott had argued, had smashed the great German offensive before it had overwhelmed Anzio's thin defenses.

Wallace Dewey thought, *The offensive always wins. I hope we Americans never forget that; Our enemies always remember—and they will in the future. Let us never forget, to our peril.*

Both armies, bleeding, drained dry of effort and supply, paused, licking their wounds. Both were exhausted. At this moment, neither had the force for final victory.

But the beachhead had been saved.

88

Part Three

Breakout

On February 19, 1944, the courage of the holding infantry and the blazing counterattack mounted by the 1st Armored Division broke the German offensive. Both Germans and Allies reeled from exhaustion. But the beachhead had reserves, and the German reserves were gone, swallowed by the flaming maw of battle.

The Allies had not won a success at Anzio—not yet. They were no nearer Rome, and they had failed to force a German withdrawal from South Italy. A campaign designed to restore mobility to the Italian front now, ironically, stalemated into long months of agony. Neither Germans nor Allies would be able to move for a long time.

But the Germans had failed, too. After holding with a daring and courageous defense, they had assembled a mighty force to drive the beachhead into the sea. Even Hitler realized that the failure to do so remained a major German disaster.

For the beachhead was in the German flank, threatening communications to the south, a potential launching place for an Allied drive on Rome. Allied strength was increasing. German strength grew less.

On either side, thirty thousand men had fallen. In dead and wounded, honors were almost even. But the German loses had been in vain, while the Allies had not lost the final decision. It had only been deferred.

For four months the long agony of Anzio would continue, from January through May, 1944. It would be hard to take. But when spring came to Italy, Fifth Army would be ready to move again . . .

8

The Long Wait

Of the six German divisions that had been in the Albano road salient February 19, 1944, none was fit for further offensive action. Fighting—bitter, bloody fighting—continued, but now the German High Command had no real hope of destroying the Anzio beachhead. Along the perimeter some of the action was dramatic and bloody.

On February 16, Lieutenant Colonel Laurence C. Brown's 2nd Battalion, 157th Infantry, 45th Division, had held a front some fifteen hundred yards wide astride the Albano road south of Carroceto. The first waves of the massive German attack overran both flanks of the battalion. All contact with adjacent units was lost. In this situation, some units would have considered surrender.

But not Colonel Brown's 2nd Battalion, 157th Infantry. It was in rugged terrain—ground with a series of caves to the west. Brown ordered a withdrawal into the caves, and there 2nd Battalion began a fight for its life.

Sergeant Booth Rawlings, former Pennsylvania State Trooper, got into the Battle of the Caves by accident. An MP, he had been on the road, checking stragglers, when Germans had punched through on each side, and there had been nothing else to do but retreat into the caves with the 2nd Battalion.

Now, sighting his rusting M-1 rifle down the ravine his squad covered, he was wondering how the devil they were going to hold out much longer.

A medium-sized, straw-haired man of twenty-five, with a serious face and a competent, deliberate way of moving, he was glad he wasn't married, because he didn't think many of these men besieged in the caves were going to get out. Wave after wave of Krauts had been pouring against the battalion—the Germans knew better than to leave a strong force in their rear—and it had been a bad three days. Once, when the 1st Armored attack disrupted the enemy, they had gotten the wounded out. But then the steel ring had closed about them again. He rubbed his bearded face, feeling the rain mist drip from his dirty fingers. He had fifteen rounds for his M-1, and when those were gone, that was it.

With the weather like it was, there was no hope of aerial supply either.

With a scrape of boots, his squad sergeant, Jorrie, sank down beside him, squinting down the ravine. "They'll be back, after dark," Jorrie grunted. The Krauts had learned they couldn't barge in against American positions in daylight, but when the light failed . . . Jorrie took off his helmet, ran a hand over his filthy, matted straight hair. He was a dark-eyed, weather-beaten man, part Indian. "Rawlings, if I catch one, you're to take the squad—"

"Nuts," Booth said. "I'm no infantryman." He moved his wet legs, groaning at the discomfort of lying in a shallow hole in the hard, cold ground.

"Hell you're not," Jorrie grunted. "You're a sergeant, and you been here three days. If you weren't a good dogface, you'd be dead. I cleared it with the lieutenant."

"Okay," Booth said. "But don't go wishing trouble on me."

"Not likely," Jorrie said, with a tight smile, and moved off. Like Booth, he was beat, hungry and miserable, but he was not whipped yet. "Don't give out no tickets now," he called back.

It was growing dark now, and night was the bad time. Booth had trouble keeping his eyes open. He kept seeing things—rocks and bushes seemed to move; he saw shadows where there were none.

Whisk-whish-whish-bram! Bram!

Kraut mortars, softening up the area again. Day or night, the Krauts kept lobbing mortars in. And the mortars were the things that got you, if you weren't careful. If they spotted you, they could drop a mortar shell in your hip pocket.

Booth huddled deeper in his rocky pit. Pretty soon now, Krauts would be pouring up this ravine, Schmeissers ready, and—*what was that?*

He heard a rifle bolt click in the next hole. Over there, PFC Jungmann had heard it, too. He took the safety off his own piece. *Okay, you bastards—*

Someone was coming up the ravine, scuffling and banging.

Booth aimed carefully into the darkness. When you had only fifteen

92

rounds, you had to let them get close. *Now!*

"Hold it, Yank! British officer—British officer!" the words rang anxiously along the ridge. "Hold your fire, Yanks—British troops coming in!"

Thank God, Booth thought. *General Templar has sent help.*

The young English subaltern crawled up to him, grinning in the murk. "Leftenant Murff, 2/7 Queens. My men are coming in behind there."

Booth could have kissed him. "Get your men up here quick, Lieutenant. The Krauts are about to start something—they've been mortaring us—"

That was the moment the Krauts chose to attack with everything they had. The dark was split by gunfire, the red flame of shell bursts, the scream of bullets. Halfway into the American lines, the British battalion was in no position to fight.

"For God's sake, come on!" Booth yelled. "Move! Move!" By ones, twos and sections, the British infantry raced past his hole, moving deeper into the caves area. But back in the direction from which they came, a big fire fight flared. The British officer, who lay beside Booth, looked back anxiously.

"Jerry's hit us in the rear—"

But Booth was firing down the ravine. He hoped they were Krauts—but when men shot at him, he could take no chances. *Brrp-Brrp!*

They were Krauts, all right. The British Stens and Brens made a different sound.

Crack! crack ! The whole squad opened up, and in the gulley a man screamed shrilly.

It was a bad hour. But while the fire fight raged along the whole perimeter, the 2/7 Queens came in. At last, the Krauts broke off their assault, but their shelling continued.

A British sergeant crawled up to Booth. Jorrie had disappeared during the fire fight, probably hit. "You're to pull out, Yanks," the Britisher said.

An American officer crawled along the line. "Let's go," he called. "One fifty-seven's pulling out. We're relieved, men. Turn over your weapons to the British—they lost all their supply and mortars, coming in. Give your food and ammo, too. They're staying, to cover us."

"Hell," Booth Rawlings said. One of the British non-coms had told him a hundred men of the 2/7 Queens were missing after the link-up. "These poor bastards are in as bad a shape as we are."

"Orders," the officer snapped. "We're taking the wounded, too."

Booth was surprised at how few American dogfaces there were. Over eight hundred men had gone into the caves, he knew. Now only a little over two hundred were coming-out. And half of these were hospital cases, by any standard you used.

Limping, crawling, fighting, decimated but unconquered, 2nd. Battalion of the 157th came out of the caves, reaching their own lines the night of February 22. They brought the injured with them, while the British covered the withdrawal.

Once, bringing up the rear, Booth Rawlings looked back. He was wondering how the British were going to get out.

Later, he learned the British never did get out. General Templar ordered the 2/6 Queens, the 2/7's sister battalion, to resupply the trapped unit. But they couldn't get through—the Germans had tightened the ring.

After dark February 23, the Krauts overran two of the 2/7's companies. Its colonel called a conference. "We've had it, lads. Break up into small groups, make it back the best way you can—and good luck."

Less than half the surviving members of 2/7 Queens made it back.

The Battle of the Caves was over. A long time later, when Booth Rawlings pinned on the blue and gold Presidential Unit Citation Badge, awarded to all who had been with 2nd Battalion in the caves, he was thinking of the men of the 2/7 Queens, who had stayed behind.

He never heard whether the men who survived got anything or not.

Now, across the Anzio perimeter, fighting died in intensity. On February 29, the Germans again pushed out from Cisterna, against the 3rd Division. The attack struck a brick wall, failed. The Allies had no strength, however, with which to counterattack.

The battle of Anzio was still stalemated.

During the evening of February 22, 1944, while the 2nd Battalion, 157th Infantry, was being relieved by the 2/7 Queens, General Mark Clark, Fifth Army Commander, called the Deputy VI Corps Commander to his CP, which was in the cellars of Prince Borghese's villa at Anzio. The square-jawed Truscott reported calmly.

Abruptly, Clark said, "You are to relieve General Lucas as Corps Commander tomorrow morning."

Truscott frowned. He reminded Mark Clark of what he had said earlier, that he didn't want the corps. He said, "The situation is more stable now. Relieving Lucas may have an unfortunate effect on other officers. Lucas has a host of friends, and they may feel he is being sacrificed to British influence. They could come to think that they'll be thrown to the wolves, too, if they get in difficulties."

Clark listened patiently, then said, "The decision is already made. But Johnny Lucas is also a friend of mine, and I'm going to see to it that he is not hurt. I'm going to appoint him Deputy Army Commander, for the time being."

There was nothing for Truscott to do, but return to his quarters with the knowledge that he would soon be in command of the beachhead.

Clark sent for Lucas and told him: "I can no longer resist the pressure from

94

both Alexander and Devers."

Alexander wanted Lucas relieved, not because of his failure to take the Alban Hills, but because Alexander thought him exhausted and defeated, and General Devers thought him tired. The relief was without prejudice.

Lucas was deeply hurt. What bothered him most was that he thought, not without truth, that he was winning something of a victory. Subdued, he returned to his quarters.

Immediately, Truscott reported to Lucas to express his regrets. Lucas greeted him warmly; he had nothing against Truscott. But Lucas was bitter toward Clark, and he blamed his relief upon the British.

This last visit between Truscott and Lucas was for Lucian Truscott one of his saddest experiences of the war. A few years later, Major General John P. Lucas would die, worn-out and bitterly hurt.

Generals, as well as privates are casualties of war.

Now Truscott was in command at Anzio, and he was one of the finest fighting generals in the Army. He took charge at once, and from this moment forward, he planned only for the breakout, for only on that day would the Anzio operation justify its cost.

But a breakout from Anzio had to be coordinated to coincide with a breakthrough on the southern Italian front. The two fronts had to link. And in the south, *Graf* von der Schulenberg's fanatical German paratroops still clung to a place called Cassino, and General Fridolin von Senger had not withdrawn Hitler's order that the *Gustavstellung* be held to the last.

At Anzio, the long wait began. In many ways, this was the worst period of all for the men on the bloody beachhead. German artillery massed. Heavy guns were dug into the slopes of the Colli Laziali, from where they ranged any gun on the beachhead. Two great 280-mm. railroad guns—"Anzio Express"or "Anzio Annie"—were brought up, and fired from railway tunnels near Campolene and Castel Gandolfo. No single inch of the beachhead was safe from German shellfire.

The *Luftwaffe* still had teeth. Nightly, there came the drone of planes, the crump of exploding bombs.

Men continued to die.

PFC Corey Hamilton, big and strong and blue-eyed, nineteen years old and not mad at anybody, arrived on the Anzio beachhead as a replacement the first week in March, 1944. The large-scale fighting might be over, but Corey, sent to help fill the frightful gaps in the 45th Division, soon learned that, in its way, position warfare can be the most horrible of all.

Along a twenty-mile perimeter, Germans and Allies faced each other, and neither side was happy about the other's being there.

All ten of the replacements who had come in with Corey were sent to

Lieutenant Howie Cresap's platoon, which held a small area that had been swampland before Mussolini drained the Pontine Marshes. Now the swamp was coming back.

That first day, when Technical Sergeant Musko, the platoon sergeant, brought them to Cresap's bunker, the platoon leader had set them straight. Cold, wet, scared and miserable in the rain, they had listened to his no-nonsense briefing.

Cresap was a well-muscled young man, brown-eyed, firm-chinned and up from the ranks. He spoke in a slight Southwestern accent. The gold bar on his collar, like the crossed muskets on the other side of the OD shirt, was a musty green. But he was clean-shaven, and his manner crisp.

He showed them the platooon area, pointing his finger down the gullies, across the bare, blasted earth. "Our lines run along here, and here, across to there. See those buildings up ahead? The Krauts are in them. From there, and from their OPs up on those hills, the Alban Hills, they can see you anytime you get out of a hole. Got that?"

The replacements got it. Now they understood why everyone at Anzio walked bent over, scuttling along like scared crabs. "The Anzio Gait," they called it. You never knew when a Kraut OP had you spotted, or a round was coming in—you only knew that sooner or later one would come in.

"The war's bogged down here," Cresap continued in his precise manner. His uniform was stained and filthy, and there were huge shadows under his eyes. But though he looked like an old man, he was only a little older than Corey Hamilton's nineteen years. "We hold our lines, the Krauts hold theirs. We patrol, so do they. The one thing we can't do is sit on our asses. The water table is high here, only a foot or so under the ground. This is bad for trench foot, but it is good in that it keeps us mobile, on our toes. We can't dig deep holes or build fancy trenches to hide in. And we've got to stay mobile, because sooner or later, we'll get orders to attack. When we start next time, we won't stop."

Cresap had paused a moment, blinking his bloodshot brown eyes wearily. Then they were sharp again. "Men, for crissakes, watch your feet. We'll get fresh socks up to you two or three times a week. Be careful. Listen to your squad sergeants; they know the score. In the meantime, remember you're members of the best damn platoon in the best damn company in the best battalion in the Army! Now get lost."

Later, Moody, a tall, rangy Texan, and Corey's best friend, had asked their squad leader, Gumpertz, "This Lieutenant Cresap a pretty good Joe?"

And Staff Sergeant Gumpertz, a bearded wrinkled, old man of twenty-eight, who had three children back in Wisconsin, spat. "Who gives a good crap? He knows his job, and you can thank God for that. What you want out of an officer is that he knows his business. The hell with the rest of it. That

96

good Joe stuff goes with the rear echelons. They got things to worry about other than stayin' alive." Gumpertz spat again, and shook his head. "An officer can't cut the mustard, he don't last long up here. Me, I wouldn't be an officer for anything they could give me."

Years later, Corey Hamilton remembered that. After the war, when the Doolittle Board was meeting, he noticed one thing: the men who were complaining about the caste system never came from the front line companies. When an officer lay in the same dirty water you did, and took twice the chances, because he had to move about, what kind of a caste system was that?

Gumpertz assigned Moody and Corey to positions in the squad, which meant they each got a hole, half-full of icy water.

So began two weeks of hell for PFC Corey Hamilton, Rifleman, 45th Division.

Corey, big and strong and blue-eyed, had played football in high school before his mother had made him quit. He had a tough, resilient body, and he had a steady nature, not the kind to get upset easily. He was to find a strong body and a mind that did not anger quickly were not enough. Not if you were only nineteen and had never had it tough before.

The first trouble came his first week, when the squad had scouted across the ravines, close to the German lines. A limited attack, just to keep the Krauts honest, Lieutenant Cresap had said. Corey had been scared as hell when he fixed his bayonet, but Moody, the lean, dark kid from Amarillo, grinned at him.

"Just a turkey shoot, Corey, old lad," the green-eyed Texan drawled. "Only difference, you can't eat Krauts, even with sauerkraut."

Nothing seemed to bother Moody, though Corey thought his face was pale, too, when they set out, after dark.

They followed Gumpertz into the gullies, stepped carefully across a small feeder creek. The fringe of brush that shielded the creek was blasted and torn; a lot of shell fire had churned this area.

Then they crawled on their hands and knees over the ridges, until they came in close to the German lines. They could hear men talking over there, in low voices. Corey heard a man laugh, deep-toned and natural.

Then Gumpertz, watching Lieutenant Cresap, waved his arm. The second squad, which was to be the base of fire, opened up on the Krauts, the BAR and M-1s, filling the night with strident noise. Behind Gumpertz, Moody and Corey and the other men crowded forward.

Blam! A German fired at Corey from a hole just in front of him. Orange-lavender streaks split the night in all directions. Somewhere, the deep-voiced Kraut was bellowing orders.

"Let 'em have it!" Gumpertz screamed. His rifle flamed again and again, from the hip. Then he wavered in the darkness, fell over.

Corey saw the indistinct shape of the German running toward Gumpertz. He saw the Kraut lift his bayoneted rifle, saw the faint gleam of the steel as it came down.

Gumpertz, as the steel pierced him, made a terrible, anguished sound. Corey, standing with his rifle in his hands, could not move. He could only stare, sickly, stupidly.

The German wheeled toward him, the bayonet, not gleaming now, whipping forward viciously. Then the Kraut cried out and went over on his back. Beside Corey's head, Moody's rifle blast had almost taken an ear off.

"Get in those Kraut holes!" Moody yelled. He disappeared into the ground, began firing into the demoralized German squad from the side. Corey tumbled after him, his rifle gripped in shaking hands. But he could not shoot. It never occurred to him to shoot.

Then, Lieutenant Cresap's whistle blast cut through the firing. "Let's make tracks!" Moody snapped. He leaped up out of the hole, bent over Gumpertz. "Dead," he said angrily. "Corey, you take him—he's too big for me!"

Corey carried Gumpertz back, losing his rifle in the process. All the way Gumpertz' blood ran down Corey's neck, under his OD shirt, until his whole torso was stained and reeking.

When they got back into their own lines, another man besides Gumpertz had been wounded. This man sat holding his stomach, moaning, while the blood bubbled through, until the medics came and carried him away.

Corey vomited for a full five minutes, before he could go back to his hole. Then he went back without his rifle, and Cresap gave him a real chewing out over that.

A few nights later, the Krauts came to pay them back. Suddenly a wave of men burst out of the ravine, screaming and shooting and hurling long, potato masher grenades. For a minute, even though they had been ready, it was touch and go for Howie Cresap's platoon.

This time Corey fired his rifle. He saw the dark, fuzzy shape of a lean German soldier blown backward by the blast, heard the man crawling about and crying out in the darkness. When the attack had been beaten off, the German raiders melting into the night under the savage hammering of the platoon's weapons and the artillery they had called down, the man Corey had shot continued to scream and moan out in front of the platoon position. Cresap's men didn't care—they had five of their own wounded to care for.

The German continued to cry out sporadically all night. None of them knew German, and they didn't know what he was saying. About an hour before dawn, he died, and the front was quiet.

That day, sweeping the area, Corey found his bullet had blasted away the attacking German's genitals, tearing, a deep hole in his crotch. Before he

98

died, the German had bit his thin lips to bloody shreds.

At that moment, in Corey Hamilton, Rifleman, something gave way.

The first time you saw a man get it, something happened to you. Especially if you had never seen death before. Inside a man there are a lot of little dams. It takes a great deal to break them all down, if the man is solid to begin with. But cold helps, and hunger, and misery, and lack of sleep. And fear. Fear helps most. And each time you see a man get it, a new little dam bursts, and you are closer to the rawness that is inside every man.

In some men, these dams are stronger than in others. They take longer to break, but if they do, there is nothing left to hold the man together.

The rain fell. The holes were always full of water. Food was C rations, cold and greasy, and who wanted hash for breakfast? And it was always cold.

Day and night, the platoon was shelled. H & I, they called it—harassment and interdiction. Both sides fired it from dark to dawn. How much interdiction was done was anyone's guess—but there was no doubt about the harassment.

Sleep Corey forgot about. Until he could doze off standing up, in the rain, with his feet in dirty water. After a few days, he found he could. And then he worried, because if he went to sleep at the wrong time, he might never wake up.

There was fear. On line, every man is afraid, has been afraid, or will be afraid, except the liars. Fear, insidious, acid, too-long prolonged, does things to a man, in time.

And men died. Not many, but one here, one there, and always bloodily, brutally, in pain and fear. Mostly, it was the new men, the replacements. The old men, the veterans, had lived to learn that sixth sense which now permitted them to survive. They heard the *click* as a mortar round went into its tube over there; they hit the ground a split second sooner. They never forgot to keep heads down. The ones who couldn't learn died.

The new squad leader, Quitman, put Moody and Corey on outpost, out in front of the main platoon position, Corey's fourteenth day on line.

Their foxholes were a few yards apart. Corey could see Moody's indistinct shape in the dark, though they could not talk. If they heard anything, it wouldn't be dark long. One call to the artillery would douse the area with parachute flares.

God, Corey thought, *I'm sleepy! I got to keep my mind on something, so I can stay awake.* One of the fellows in the third squad had showed him how to rig up a bayonet under his chin, so that the point pricked him when he nodded. But Corey hated the sight of a bayonet. He could still hear Gumpertz' scream, feel his warm blood down his back. He shuddered.

He didn't seem able to think about girls any more, and vaguely, this worried him.

Back at Benning, even when his young body was tired from slogging along Hour Glass Road and Black Hawk Trail, at night he dreamed of women. Hell, he even thought of girls while he was running the obstacle course!

He tried to think of Elizabeth, his girl back home. It was hard to think of her—even though he had her letters in his pocket. Her letters, when they came, now and then, were nuttier than ever. *I don't mind your not making OCS, she had written, because privates do all the fighting, anyway. You know dear, you have never said anything about medals—have you won any yet?*

Corey Hamilton felt giddy. He shook his head to clear it.

He remembered his mother's last letter. *Don't get your feet wet, you know how it always gives you a cold.*

It had been a mistake, writing his mother. Now he had her all worried, because he had said it rained a lot. If she were here, she'd be raising hell. She had always raised hell, with his Dad, with the high school principal, with the dean at college before the draft got him. He wondered idly how much hell Lieutenant Cresap would take, if his Mom got hold of him. *Not very much,* he decided.

Pop! A flare burst whitely, throwing wavering light over the blighted area across the gully. Somebody was nervous in the next platoon. *Buckabuckabuckabuck.* That was a friendly machine gun; the Kraut guns had a higher cyclic rate.

He thought of Elizabeth, her firm, tanned skin against white sheets, holding a bottle of fresh milk. He wondered which he'd take first, the fresh milk or Elizabeth, then decided he'd just go to sleep on the clean sheets.

Then he thought about his mother coming out here to raise hell with Howie Cresap, and he started to laugh. He laughed, and laughed, until he felt a tear trickle down his fuzzy cheek.

Mrs. George Hamilton couldn't do much about Lieutenant Cresap. She might push Dad around, but not the lieutenant!

Spang!

There was old Joe, the friendly sniper, again. That lousy Kraut had been trying to plug somebody for a week. Corey hadn't heard the bullet pass, so he must have shot at Moody. Corey hunched lower in his hole, shifting his numb feet in the icy water.

He wished he could take off his boots, but he knew he'd never get his feet back in them again. *Change your socks, his mother had said. What the hell good does that do, Mother, since I have to put my feet back in the water again? Huh?*

He began to laugh again, this time out loud.

That was pretty good; he'd have to tell it to old Moody.

Moody would get a kick out of it; Moody, with his drawl, and his calm, cool, green eyes, was quite a boy. Nothing ever bothered Moody—Moody said that was because of the inherent superiority of Texan manhood."

100

"Hey, Moody," he whispered. "You awake?"

Moody didn't answer. In the dark, Corey could see Moody's head leaning forward, his chin blending into the front of his dirty field jacket.

Corey sloshed out of his hole and crawled the six yards to Moody's position. He grabbed Moody's shoulder. "Hey!"

Moody's head fell forward. Even in the murky light, Corey saw the gaping ruin where Moody's jaw had been, the white teeth gaping skull-like from the frothy horror. The sniper's bullet had ripped most of the lower face away.

Inside Corey Hamilton, Rifleman, the last tiny dam broke, all at once. He ran screaming and crying all the way back to the platoon.

Corporal Bran Brainerd, a small man with a pug nose and tough, lined face, brought the big fellow, Hamilton, to the aid station. He was thinking, *If they'd shoot a few more of these damn psychos, there wouldn't be so many around.*

"Come on," he snapped. His rough voice was out of the southern Indiana hills, and he moved with a farmer's deliberate gait.

The big fellow just looked at him. But at least he had quit bawling. Brainerd shoved him inside the dugout that served as battalion aid station. They said that Hamilton had sat at the company CP for a solid hour, bawling and raising hell over someone called Moody.

"Another one for you, Doc," Bran said to the first lieutenant, who was drinking a steaming cup of coffee. You didn't have to worry about medical officers; they didn't give a damn about rank, like some officers Bran knew.

The surgeon moved forward. "Where are you hit, son?"

"He ain't," Brainerd said. "He's a damn faker."

The doctor took the big man's shoulder, wheeled him over to the light of the Coleman lantern. He took something and looked into the big blond kid's eyes.

The kid wouldn't say anything at all.

"How long's he been on line? You know?" The medical officer snapped at Brainerd. "Is he brand-new, or has he been around?"

"I remember when he come in. About two weeks ago," Bran told the medic.

The young surgeon rubbed his face. "Combat-induced," he muttered. "Well, you don't get much of the other kind up here—the men who were psychoneurotic when they came in the Army get weeded out in training."

"Well, does he get a Section Eight?" Bran asked.

The doctor looked at Bran sharply. "He'll be all right. All he needs is rest. I'll send him back to the port hospital—though God knows there isn't much rest to be found there."

"Ought to shoot a few of 'em, Doc," Bran said. "They're faking."

The medical lieutenant said, "That's enough, Corporal." Then, angrily, he said, "Look, Brainerd. All men are not alike. Their backgrounds—when did

101

you first see blood?"

"Shoot," Brainerd said. "My Maw used to get me to pull chicken heads off when I was five or six, afore she plucked 'em. They'd flop and throw blood all over the place. Ever see a chicken with its head pulled off?"

"No, but I've seen worse," the lieutenant muttered. "And I suppose your old man belted you a few times now and then?"

Bran grinned. "Hell, yes!"

"You realize some of these kids never saw blood in their lives before they came out here? This kid—" he looked at the dog tags—Hamilton, his mother probably tucked him into bed every night. I don't see how some of them stand it so long."

He filled out a tag and pinned it on Hamilton's field jacket, which was covered with blood.

Corporal Brainerd went back into the dark. He turned once and looked back into the dugout. *Still oughta shoot 'em, he thought. What do these New York doctors know about it?*

Corey remembered getting back to the hospital. Most of all he remembered the sheets. Clean, white sheets. But he couldn't sleep. He just lay and shook sometimes, until the doctor gave him something.

He kept seeing Moody, with his head blown off.

Once, he heard two doctors talking. One was upset about the rate of psychoneurosis that was showing up on the beachhead. "There's something wrong with the whole generation! No excuse for this. We ought to do like the Russian Army—do you know they don't officially recognize battle fatigue?"

"Then they're blind," the other doctor snapped. "They've got it, too, even though they have a different kind of population, bred a hell of a lot tougher than ours. They just don't give a damn about the individual."

"Maybe we pay too much attention to the individual, in a war like this—"

"So now you want us to be like the Nazis, bring up our boys prepared to die for the *Vaterland*? Is that it? That the kind of conditioned, brainless, insensitive individual you want to produce? Listen, Stein, there are other values besides the military—"

The two doctors moved off, and Corey could not hear them any more.

All the time he was in the hospital, Corey could hear the shells come in. The Krauts kept plastering the port area. He heard the snorting roar, then the sort of whizzing sound as Anzio Annie came in. Every so often, the ground shook.

New men kept coming into the hospital all the time. But Corey knew the Nazis wouldn't shell the hospital. There were rules against that.

The American field hospital area wasn't dug in. It stood in bare fields

102

about a mile east of Nettuno, with the red crosses plainly visible to the enemy observers. Shells went over the hospital daily, but none had dropped close.

On March 22, the third day of Corey's stay, it happened.

Early in the morning, the shells screamed into the hospital. One shell ripped into Corey's tent and struck the stove, exploding at bed level. There were fifty men in the tent.

The other shells, fifty or sixty of them, plastered the area. They were 88s, high-explosive, anti-personnel projectiles.

Five patients in Corey's tent died. Eleven others had new wounds. The nurse was the worst of all. She clutched at her breast and went to her knees. When they got to her, she was dead.

Several doctors, more nurses and a dozen corpsmen were hit. The hospital was in a sort of panic, with the wounded men screaming from their beds.

"Get us out of here! Get us out of here!" the helpless men cried. Corey went stumbling into the shambles. He saw the young, short-haired nurse sprawled on the floor of the tent, her breast a bright smear of blood; he saw the patients, with the blood of fresh wounds streaming through their bandages, screaming and trying to move about.

Corey began to shake. He could feel the tremors start in his legs. The doctor and the corpsmen who had been untouched were running about, in something like panic.

Bram-Bram-Bram! A new stonk of explosive shells roared in, shaking the tent with mud and steel fragments.

A nurse, gray hair flying, ran into Corey, almost knocking him down. She looked at his strong body, free of bandages, and snapped, "Here! Give me a hand, soldier! Get these men back into their beds!"

She wasn't panicked; she was mad, her eyes napping, as hard as the brass leaf on her collar. Corey suddenly felt the tremors halt, felt the cool reason sweep into him. Hell, he'd been on the line; head been shot at before.

"Yes, ma'am," he said.

He turned, grabbed one of the corpsmen who was jittering about, still shocked. "Here—help me with these men on the floor."

The corpsman went with him. Together, they lifted half a dozen moaning men back to their cots. The seventh man was dead, but they put him in his bed anyway. More doctors arrived, and the medical officers took charge, bringing some order to the chaos. The wounded were treated, the dead carried out. Corey was too busy to think.

The shelling ceased, and General Truscott, the beachhead commander, came into the tent. His face was grim and his jaw was set. The same chief nurse who had bumped into Corey marched up to him. She waved a huge, jagged shell fragment under the general's nose.

"General, these came through my tent while I was in bed. We can't take

103

care of our patients unless we can get some rest around here. What are you going to do about it?"

The men in the wards were crying out to Truscott, recognizing his bright leather jacket, "General! Get us out of here! For God's sake, let us go back to the front. We're better off up there!"

General Truscott was mad, too—and sick, looking at the carnage wreaked on the already injured bodies of the men who had been in the hospital. But all he could do was to say he'd have corps artillery counterbattery every spot from which the Germans could fire on the hospital, and to order the hospital dug in a foot or two. Below that level, there was water.

Corey would never forget the gallantry of the Army nurses, who from that day forward worked under intermittent shelling. For the shelling of the tents with red crosses was deliberate, and repeated. But Corey did not stay there to see it. At noon, Corey Hamilton, battle fatigue casualty, went to the surgeon and said, "I'm ready to return to my unit."

It had taken only a little rest, after all. Under the broken dams, the man was solid. Corey Hamilton, Rifleman, would not break again.

9

The Road to Rome

"The capture of Rome is the only important objective!"—General Mark Wayne Clark to Lucian Truscott at Anzio, May 6, 1944.

In the hour before dawn, May 23, 1944, Generals Lucian Truscott, Mark Clark and a few staff officers gathered in an artillery OP near the front lines before Cisterna. Light rain had fallen, but a few stars gave promise of a clear day. The entire front was strangely quiet.

Against the northern sky, Truscott thought he could see the menacing outline of the Colli Laziali, but he could not be sure. Closer, nothing moved. There was nothing to indicate that 150,000 men of the U.S. VI Corps stood tensely waiting the command to attack.

Days before, in the south, the Italian front had broken wide-open. Fifth Army had advanced across the hills, carrying the German divisions before it, and the Polish Corps with the Eighth Army had taken Cassino. But the Germans were not fleeing; they were retreating subbornly, fighting for each meter of the way. However, they were retreating, and the time seemed ripe for the final blow to be struck. It would come against the German flank, from the Anzio beachhead.

Clark, who wanted Rome so badly now he could taste it, had preferred to attack to the northwest, across the Colli Laziali, on the shortest route to the Eternal City. But the over-all commander, Alexander, had insisted that the attack from the beachhead strike east, to Cisterna and then to the Valmontone Gap, where VI Corps had a good chance of cutting off the retreat of von Vietinghoff's Tenth Army.

Clark had gone along, but he had told Truscott to be prepared to shift the attack toward Rome at any time, on orders. Now, the blow was ready to fall.

In the OP, Lucian Truscott could feel the tension. His staff was silent. The minute hands of the synchronized watches ticked slowly toward H-Hour.

Once before they had tried to break out of Anzio, and they had got a bloody nose. Thirty thousand bloody noses, to be exact. But now, VI Corps was immeasurably stronger, and the Germans should be weaker.

Truscott looked down at his watch one last time. 0545! Time for the artillery to open up. He thought, in the last minute of silence, *for better or for worse, the die is cast.*

This time, there would be no stopping.

Lieutenant Erich von Fehrenteil moved quietly through the battered streets of Cisterna. In this hour before daylight, as commanding officer of Number 3 Company, 715th Division, he should be with his company on the other side of the Mussolini Canal. But for so long now, nothing had happened. The Amis had not been active for months, and there was no reason why he should not visit his friends in Cisterna.

He was a brunet, clear-eyed young man of twenty-four, who looked thirty. Now he shook his head, trying to clear it of the wine fumes of the night before. Damn it, he hadn't planned to stay up all night!

But today he would do nothing more than watch the Amis play another game of baseball. He had seen them play more than once, through his good Zeiss glasses. A silly game but better than the game of killing each other. Even here, where you faced the enemy at close range day after day, you could not fight forever. For some time now, there had been a sort of gentleman's agreement.

Don't shoot at me, Ami, and I'll not shoot at you.

He looked at his watch. Damn it, he would have to hurry. 0545, May 23. But a day like any other day. So he didn't make it; Stransky was there. Stransky could handle anything from muster to an attack. The German NCO, with his attention to duty, was the best in the world.

Lightning flashes in the west, a crash of thunder. *Rain,* he thought. Then from the west, the world turned to light, and the air screamed, split by the roar of more than a thousand big guns. A solid wall of fire erupted in the German lines out there, while the sky was streaked with the eerie pattern of machine-gun tracer. The earth itself shook.

Fehrenteil knew what this meant. *Attack!* Flame blossomed in front of him, a section of stone wall collapsed slowly. He began to run, toward his company across the Mussolini Canal. Then he stopped. He knew he would never make it now.

He ran back through the flashes and screaming steel to the 128 Panzer Grenadiers Command Post. Inside there was confusion, stunned unbelief, as men and officers milled around.

Overhead, in the first rays of the sun, the silvery wings of Ami fighter bombers glinted evilly. The din of their screaming engines was horrible as they came over the town. Three waves of fighters—then the bombers dropped their loads. Inside Cisterna, it was shrieking hell, and towering columns of smoke rose.

A bomb hit the CP. Two sergeants were groaning in the ruins. But there was no safety outside; the terrible Ami artillery Fehrenteil had first experienced so long ago crashed in continually.

For forty minutes the big guns fired, while German artillery, counterbatteried into silence, stood helplessly by. Then the barrage ceased. In the sudden, deafening silence, almost more terrible than the barrage, Fehrenteil thought, *Here they come. I will never reach my company now.*

Second Lieutenant Harry S. Bonsal's platoon went in early, soon after the artillery stopped blasting the Kraut positions up ahead. Once again 3rd Division had drawn the nasty one, he thought—artillery and planes or not, Cisterna was going to be a nasty one. He knew its strength from the old days, when 3rd Division had tried to take it in February.

He was an officer now, not a sergeant, but putting the bars on your collar didn't make it any easier. It made it harder, for now he felt he had to try a little more.

Watch that kind of thinking, Harry, he told himself, *that's what gets you scragged.* Harry Bonsal had seen the second looies come and go, and it wasn't an entirely comfortable feeling to realize he'd been made one himself.

Up ahead, a pall of dust from the shelling and bombing obscured the entire front. Maybe that was just as well; the Krauts couldn't see you.

"Let's go!" he said, and waved the platoon forward. In front of the infantry, tanks clanked and roared into the dust swirls. Bonsal and his platoon had to run to keep up with them.

Shocked, the Krauts seemed to be floundering about in the smoke and dust. They couldn't see to shoot, but they were firing their weapons anyway. Harry's men and the tanks were on top of them before they realized their danger.

Harry kept ahead of his men, spraying a full magazine from his carbine into the Kraut-fortified positions. *To hell with hand to hand.* He slapped a fresh magazine into the carbine. *I don't intend to get in that close again.* He hunched over before a big M-4 tank, followed its deliberate crunching through the Kraut dugouts. The Krauts had really fortified Cisterna. The ravines and canals on both sides of town had been revetted and entrenched, and German machine-gun emplacements were everywhere.

But the Germans had been taken by surprise by the crushing barrage that preceded Harry Bonsal's attack. In front of the lumbering M-4 tank, three men ran from a dugout. Even in the smoke and haze Harry could see they were half-dressed, without boots and helmetless.

The tank fired into them with its machine guns. A man cried out and fell. The others screamed and ran. Harry brought down one with his carbine; his platoon sent a storm of rifle fire after the other. The man fell into a canal, kicking and threshing.

The tank engines were roaring, its guns chattering. More Germans ran out of the dugouts and entrenchments—but these were dropping rifles, throwing away helmets. Their hands were in the air.

The prisoners made Harry nervous. "Somebody take 'em back," he ordered, watching the dazed, huddled captives warily. One of his men waved an   M-1; the prisoners seemed only too eager to move toward the American lines.

In the smoke and dust, the German artillery spotters couldn't see to fire. On both sides, the big guns remained quiet, while the infantry fought and clawed its way through the German defenses.

Not all the defenders surrendered. From a revetment a machine gun opened up on Harry's platoon. *Brrrrp-brrrrp!* He saw Sergeant Arthur, a squad leader, stumble and fall, grabbing at his shattered leg.

Harry took the phone attached to the rear of the tank and spoke into the supporting M-4's intercom. "Get in there and squash that gun."

"Can't, Lieutenant," came the tanker's tinny voice. "We can't get across the canals."

It was true. All along the line the heavy tanks were being stopped. "Support me by fire then," Harry snapped, and put the phone back. "Kovalics!"

"Here, sir!" The bulky squad leader squatted down beside Harry in the shelter of the tank's steel hull.

"Take your squad and flank those machine guns up ahead. You go right— I'll take Arthur's squad to the left. We'll catch them between us."

"Right, sir!" You didn't have to draw a picture for Kovalics.

Harry pounded through the smoking debris, bent low, eight men strung out behind him. They went across a canal, splashing in the water, while the German gunners tried to center on them. When the gun fired, they hit the ground. They they got up and raced on again. A minute later, they were piling into a small ravine fifty yards to the left of the two gun nests.

Harry took out a grenade. "Let's go!" he yelled. He ran forward, seeing the startled gunner swing the MG 42 to cover him. He threw the grenade with all his strength.

He didn't hear the machine gun, but something struck him a solid blow just below the hip. He tried to take a step forward, and fell. He got up—there was no pain. He tried to run again, and again he fell. The damn leg was broken. "Go on—go on!" he screamed at his men.

They pushed forward, shooting and killing the gunners Harry's grenade had dazed and wounded.

Now the pain came to Harry Bonsal—raw and violent. He gasped, but lying in the dust, hearing the shooting swelling to the west, as the 3rd Division went into Cisterna, he could not help thinking, *It's a million-dollar wound. This time, I'll go back. Two Purple Hearts, and I'm still alive.*

Harry lifted himself up, trying to see his men's advance. Kovalics had the platoon now, and he was a good man. Maybe they'd never given him the bars—Kovalics had never finished school—but he knew how to take care of the men. Harry was glad of that, because the fighting wasn't finished.

For the ancient town of Cisterna was an obstacle. On high ground up from the Pontine Marshes, its stone houses and narrow rubble-strewn streets were formidable. Each house had a deep wine cellar which could be defended. The dust was clearing now, and Harry could see the rail line leading west. It threw up a steep embankment; the Krauts would defend along that. They didn't have Cisterna yet.

Behind the German lines, Harry could see the steep rise of the Alban Hills, seven miles beyond. At the foot of those hills nestled the old Roman town of Velletri, shining in the warm May sun like an antique medallion. And beyond that, a good fifteen miles away, lay Valmontone.

We'll have to take those towns, Harry thought. Velletri would crack the German Caesar line; the capture of the Valmontone Gap would trap the remnants of the German Tenth Army retreating from the south.

The pain flooded up his side now, making his nerves scream when he tried to move; the shock was wearing off. He gasped and sank back, waiting for the medic. *We'll have to take those towns, but someone else will have to do it.*

With any luck at all, Mrs. Bonsal's boy Harry was going home.

Late in the afternoon of May 25, General Lucian Truscott was returning to his command post at Conca with a feeling of elation.

His methodical mind was reviewing the events of the last two days. The offensive was going well. They were going to break out. But it had not been easy.

The 3rd Division had first surrounded Cisterna, cutting around it like a knife cuts around the bad spot in an apple. Then they had gone in and taken it, street by street. It had been a dirty, bloody business, but now they had it, at last.

Harman's 1st Armored Division, to the left of the 3rd, had battered its way across Feminamorta Creek, cracking the German lines. On the far right, the intense, driving Brigadier General Frederick's American and Canadian 1st Special Service Force had fought through to Highway 7, although it had been heavily attacked by Tiger tanks.

The 45th, holding the line to the northwest, had thrown back strong German counterattacks. More than fifteen hundred German prisoners had been taken in two days.

Now Harmon's armor was probing toward Velletri, a key communication center in the German line. The fall of Velletri could turn the key to Rome, Truscott knew. And an armored task force under Colonel Hamilton Howze had crossed the valley east of Velletri, to the Cori-Artena road. Just ahead lay Valmontone and apparently, the Germans had nothing there to defend it.

Late in the afternoon of May 25, Truscott could honestly feel a certain jubilation. With his advance pressing past Cisterna, VI Corps would be astride the German line of withdrawal at Valmontone no later than next morning. Tenth German Army, or at least large parts of it, was trapped!

But this was not to be. In the CP at Conca, Brigadier General Donald W. Brann, Mark Clark's Operations Officer, was waiting for Truscott. As Truscott heard his new orders, his former elation faded.

The day before, Clark had asked Truscott if he had considered changing the direction of attack from Valmontone to the northwest, the direct route to Rome. Truscott had said, yes, he had thought of it—but only for one reason. If the enemy should become alarmed at the acute threat to his communications and shift forces from the fortified Colli Laziali sector toward Valmontone, then it might be better to attack to the northwest.

If I Parachute Corps, the crack German troops defending Velletri and the Colli Laziali, moved to Valmontone, they could probably delay VI Corps long enough to allow von Vietinghoff's Tenth Army to escape the trap.

So Truscott had said, if the Germans started to withdraw any forces on the northwest perimeter of the beachhead, then he figured the best thing to do would be to shift the Allied attack across the Alban Hills, to try to cut off the fleeing Tenth Army north of them, rather than at Valmontone.

Clark then told Truscott to keep such a plan up to date. Truscott knew that Clark's mind was never far from Rome.

The British Eighth Army was pushing up the Liri Valley, and Clark, who very much felt Fifth Army should have the honor, was afraid the British might be first in Rome. And Clark wanted Rome now, not next month. Like all senior officers in the Mediterranean, he knew Eisenhower's Second Front would open any day. When that happened, Italy, and the efforts of Fifth Army, would be relegated to the back page.

With each hour's delay by the stubborn Germans, Clark had become more impatient. Finally, on May 25, the impatience showed.

For General Brann told Truscott, as he came into the CP, "The Boss wants you to leave the 3rd Infantry Division and the Special Service Force to block Highway 6 and mount that assault you discussed with him to the northwest as soon as you can."

Truscott was dumfounded.

"The time is not right now," he protested. "We have no evidence of any withdrawal from the western part of the beachhead, and none of any German concentration in Valmontone except some recon elements of the Herman Göring Division. My agreement with Clark was based on those assumptions. This is no time to shift the attack—we should pour our maximum power into the Valmontone Gap to insure destruction of the retreating German Army."

Then he said, "I won't comply with this order without talking first to General Clark in person!"

Brann shrugged. He said Clark had left the beachhead and could not be reached even by radio. He repeated, "General Clark ordered the attack northwest."

There was nothing to do but change the direction of attack.

At 1555 General Brann radioed Clark that Truscott was entirely in accord with Fifth Army's plan. This was the command decision that turned the main effort of VI Corps from the Valmontone Gap and prevented the destruction of the German Tenth Army. Controversy still clings to it. General Truscott's memoirs reveal he never favored it, whatever was put in the operation journals.

While the effort of VI Corps was being diverted toward Rome, General Sir Harold Alexander was not informed of Fifth Army's change in plans. By the decision to strike northwest for Rome through the Alban Hills, Clark in effect completely changed Alexander's whole scheme of maneuver. Yet nothing was said to the Allied Army Group Commander until fifteen minutes after the new attack jumped off, 1115 hours, May 26.

Then Clark sent General Gruenther, his Chief of Staff, to inform and brief Alexander. By this time the decision was irrevocable.

Major General Gruenther, brilliant as a polished diamond, was respected and liked by Alexander; Clark could not have found a better advocate. Gruenther explained that Clark felt the enemy was disintegrating in front of Anzio. Therefore a small force could continue on to Valmontone, while the main effort cut through northwest to Rome.

It must be remembered that, while Italy and the Mediterranean had been designated a British theater of responsibility, British over-all command was not and could not be absolute. A member of Churchill's staff, Harold

Macmillan, had summed up the British position neatly during a visit to North Africa.

"We are," he had told the assembled British brass, "the Greeks in this new Roman Empire." The Americans—the new Romans—had the men, the money and the matériel; they would, in the end, do what they saw fit to do. The best the British could hope for was that, like the ancient Greeks, they might help to "educate"these new Romans.

So whatever Alexander thought of Clark's decision, he was very decent to Gruenther, who had been handed a hot potato. He said, "I'm sure the Army Commander will continue to push toward Valmontone. If the Anzio Force could capture the high ground north of Velletri, it would put the enemy at a serious disadvantage. . . . It would practically assure the success of the bridge-head attack."

Sir Harold, who knew how to be a Greek in this new Roman Empire, was accepting a *fait accompli* like the gentleman he was. After all, Fifth Army had been scoring tremendous success in the south, and he had no grounds to question Clark's judgment to act in his own zone. He acquiesced.

As it happened, the decision to strike northwest neither turned the key in the lock to Rome quickly, nor did it cut the enemy's rear at Valmontone. Kesselring, who had been worried over the situation at the Valmontone Gap, could relax very slightly. For along the Caesar Line below the Colli Laziali, from Lanuvio to Velletri, the three veteran divisions of I Parachute Corps, unknown to Allied intelligence, were waiting.

Sergeant Roger LeMarais, three-striper and tank commander, was dead tired. And he was stiff and sore, because he never quite got used to getting banged around inside a tank. Tank hulls and turrets were steel, and men were flesh—in Roger's case, very considerable flesh—and when they collided it was no contest. Roger rubbed his sore shoulder and groaned.

He was a big man, Roger LeMarais, and since tankers rode, he had never completely worn down his large belly. Not that it got in his way—he could get out of a burning tank as fast as the next guy. He rubbed his skinned elbow and frowned at the four men of his crew, closing in around him. His close-cropped, thick hair was very dark, and he sprouted a florid mustache. The lip hair made him look older than his twenty-two years, as did the foul *Italiano* cigars he smoked whenever he could get them.

Now he got ready to do a good sell job on the crew, before they struck out this morning of May 26. It was all the same, briefing your men or selling used cars on Joe's lot in Fresno, California. The man who could talk got by.

"It goes like this," he told the waiting men, leaning against the hard front sponson of the Sherman. "Task Force Howze, of which H Company, 3rd Battalion, 13th Armored Regiment—that's us—is a part, is still going to attack

112

toward Valmontone. For some reason, the brass is worried about the place. I get the idea that Colonel Howze and Colonel Cairns, our Battalion CO, are pretty mad this morning, because Corps took away a lot of the troops that were with us yesterday. We're still going to Valmontone, but now we're what the Old Man calls a 'secondary effort.' "

"I'll take a back seat in the rear row any time," grinned Kidwell, the tank gunner. "Hell, I'll even go home, if they want."

"Knock it, you clown," LeMarais said. "The main corps attack has been changed to Campoleone and Lanuvio, over in the 34th Division's zone. They say that's the quickest way to Rome."

"I'm for that," PFC Kennedy, the tall, thin assistant driver yelped. "We're outa *vino*, and that's where they got the Dago red."

"Okay," Roger continued. "But we're still going to push to the Valmontone Gap today, to cut off some Krauts. The 3rd Division's coming with us."

"Nuts," Kennedy said. "Them dogfaces ain't going to keep up. I seen 'em—they been shot to hell and gone around Cisterna, and they're tired. If the brass wants Valmontone, they'd better get some fresh troops."

Kennedy couldn't keep his big yap shut, LeMarais thought. That's why he'd never make anything higher than PFC. "All right, mount up and turn 'em over," he said.

Lieutenant Colonel Bogardus S. Cairns' battalion of medium tanks moved out. They had already punched through the main German defenses the day before, and there weren't many Krauts around this hilly, pine and cedar-covered terrain. Behind the tanks marched the 1st Battalion of the 6th Armored Infantry, on foot. It was pretty badly chewed up already.

And somewhere back there was the advance guard of the 3rd Division, which was supposed to be supporting them—or was it the other way around? Roger LeMarais couldn't remember. In this screwy division it was up and go all the time, until you couldn't remember what the hell you'd been told. That was why armor never pitched tents, like the doughfeet did, even in the rain. Armor was always getting orders to bug out somewhere.

Advancing along the road through the hills behind Cisterna, Colonel Howze sent Cairns an order to move a company of tanks to cut the Artena-Velletri road. Cairns detached I Company to set up a roadblock. Later, LeMarais heard how they'd passed a dump of *Nebelwerfer* ammo and shot it up. Big deal!

His company, H, continued along the Giulianello-Artena road. Damn, you needed to be a native to know how to say that! Back home in California, LeMarais had gone with an Italian girl once. Damn nice kid, with the prettiest hind quarters he'd ever seen—but her old man raised hell if you hadn't got in by midnight. Those Italians raised their families different from Americans. The papa was the boss.

They were passing through terraced vineyards now, and it sure looked a lot like California. Not the part where LeMarais was born, out in the desert, but like it was near the coast, where they grew the wine. Felt like home, too, cold nights, days hot and dry.

Whap! Crack-crack-crack! Whang! Small arms fire! LeMarais ducked inside the turret. He pushed the lever that swiveled the electric turret, peering through the vision slits. In the woods to his right, a hundred yards away, he saw gun flashes and a wisp of smoke. The tank ahead of his opened fire, spraying the woods with machine-gun slugs.

"Doughs!" LeMarais barked over the intercom. "Kraut infantry in the woods."

Kennedy, the BOG, opened up with the bow thirty. But that damned machine-gun was ball-mounted, and Kennedy couldn't hit the side of a barn with it.

Now, Kidwell, the gunner, was firing off short, accurate bursts with the coaxial machine gun. He could see the Kraut infantry through his periscope sight. Meanwhile, Carson, the driver had braked the big Sherman.

"Keep moving," LeMarais snapped. "Driver, move out!"

The Sherman left the road and clanked toward the brush where the Krauts lay, firing. Two more tanks followed. Over Roger's radio came the sharp command: "Stay outside the trees."

"Yes, sir," Roger said into his mike. In woods, tanks were vulnerable to bazookas and grenades, Molotov cocktails, anything. In the open, it was a different story. A tank could throw a hell of a lot of fire.

Brrrap-brrap-brrap! Kennedy and Kidwell were shooting up the woods but good. They were hitting some Krauts—the German fire was slackening. But the Krauts were pulling out, fading back into the trees. And the tanks could not follow.

That was the trouble with Italy. There wasn't any place you could take a tank off the roads. It was either wet in winter, and muddy, or now, in summer, you were up in the hills, in rocks and woods!

But some of the Germans hadn't run—they hadn't figured on the tanks coming after them. Now they got up too late, tried to pass back into the trees. *Wow-wow-wow-wow!* Slicing machine-gun bursts from Kidwell's coaxial thirty cut them down. Roger saw three men fall. One tried to get up. again. *Buck-a-buck!* Kidwell pressed the trips again, pounded the stricken Kraut into the grass.

From back in the trees, rifle and automatic fire slashed at the Sherman's hull. *Whang! Whanng!* They could shoot till doomsday, Roger thought. It'd take more than a can opener to peel old *Happy Harlot,* his tank.

New orders were crisp in his earphone. "The enemy's pulling back—back on the road—leave the doughfeet for our own infantry—proceed to Artena."

114

Back on the road again, Roger's tank roared toward Artena. Colonel Cairns ordered George Company out on the flank. In the early afternoon, both companies had rolled almost into Artena, a small stone-hutted village.

The infantry should be moving around the tanks now, going into the town. There were mines on the approaches, and German soldiers in the houses. But the infantry was nowhere in sight.

Where the hell were the doughfeet?

"I told you," PFC Kennedy said dolefully. "Them boys is tired. They couldn't keep up with no tanks."

Without foot troops, H Company's tanks couldn't take the village. "Shoot a few rounds into it," Roger ordered. Kidwell squinted into his telescopic sight.

Blam! The 75-mm. gun roared, and smoke spurted up from inside Artena. *That'd show them, anyway.* Then Roger's captain was on the air, saying he'd had orders to leave Artena for the doughfeet behind the column. H Company was to swing wide and cut Highway 6 east of Valmontone.

Happy Harlot and her sister tanks roared back onto the road. But now the 3rd Battalion had gone so far inland that the S-3 was off his maps. No one knew exactly where they were, in relation to the coast or Valmontone, but still the old M-4s clanked ahead, over winding, up-and-down roads.

Once in a while they drew a little rifle fire. They saw no enemy.

Then, just ahead, Roger saw a town, gleaming white in the later afternoon sun. That must be Valmontone itself. He leaned forward in the turret, field glasses to his nose.

Blam! Blam! Crrash!

The M-4 just in front of *Happy Harlot* slued, ran into the ditch. Colored flames danced hotly from its open turret hatch. Three men of its crew scrambled for safety, piling into the ditch. Up the hillside, a Kraut machine gun opened up on them.

Wham! Another M-4 stopped, burst into flame. The crew of this one didn't make it to the ditch. It burned for a few seconds, then exploded, blowing flame and smoke high in the air from its turret hatch.

The radio was full of combat orders, fire commands. H Company, under both artillery and AT gunfire, pecked at by small arms, fought back viciously.

"Gunner!" Roger bawled into his intercom. "H E! Right front! Antitank—eight hundred—fire!" He heard the long 75-mm. shell rasp home, heard the breech close. Kidwell was swinging the turret, pointing the big rifle.

"On the wayyyy!"

Blam! A ball of yellow-green fire blossomed at the tip of *Happy Harlot's* gun; Roger felt the warm breath of the muzzle blast flow against his drooping, mustache.

He saw the red burst in the distance, right on the at gun position. "Target!" he shouted; keeping his glasses on the hillside. "Clobber the son of a

115

bitch!" If a tanker hated anything, it was AT guns.

Blam! Blam!

The long, low 77-mm. AT gun was blasted into scrap metal; its crew lay limply across the twisted barrel. Roger LeMarais choked on the acrid fumes rising from the turret. Cordite always affected him this way. A little more firing, and he'd be sick.

All around him, tanks were moving forward along the road, stopping now and again to fire their big guns, hammering the light forces of the Herman Göring Division. H Company was on the outskirts of Valmontone, and it could punch a way in for the supporting infantry.

But where the hell were the doughfeet?

It took combined arms, the infantry-armor-artillery team, to take and hold ground. A half-assed effort by a few tanks, wasn't going to capture Valmontone through the Velletri Gap, Roger knew. And even if they went in with the tanks, Task Force Howze couldn't stop the Germans that were supposed to be coming up from the south—not alone, anyway.

But the armor had outrun the ability of the 3rd Division infantry to support and exploit it. At dusk, still fighting, Companies H and G pulled back toward Artena and formed a perimeter. Deep in enemy country, they were in for a bad night.

As he checked his pistol, and settled back in his turret to watch the open ground surrounding the perimeter, Sergeant LeMarais hoped the boys who were heading northwest, toward Velletri, were having better luck

10

The Turn of the Key

"On the standards of the 36th proudly inscribe 'Velletri.'"—Title of a story filed by Eric Sevareid, CBS Correspondent, June 1, 1944

Captain William P. Condett, now S-3—Operations Officer—1st Battalion, 141st Infantry, 36th Division, arrived at Anzio beachhead May 22, 1944 with thin little lines of bitterness around his mouth. The slaughter on the Rapido River in January had put iron into him, as it had in all the dogfaces of the Texas Division. Ever since it had arrived in Italy, the 36th had been kicked around, had its nose bloodied.

But if you grind a division long enough, you either break it, so that it is useless, or you make it veteran, with iron in its soul. Thirty-sixth Division hadn't broken.

The first night 1st Battalion camped in woods three miles northeast of Anzio. A little artillery came in, nothing bad. The bad part was having to listen to all the comments and jibes about Johnny-come-latelies and "the old corps"the Anzio veterans kept throwing at them. *You should have been here when*—and all that stuff.

The line divisions had already moved out, attacking to break out of the beachhead. Behind them they left their areas littered with signs: "Eleanor Never Slept Here," "Golden Gate, 47191/4 Miles," "Good Eats Café"and "Beach Head Hotel, Special Rates to New Arrivals." Some of the new replacements in the 36th thought the signs were very funny.

To the old hands, like Willie Condett who had been around since the first, nothing was very funny any more.

Then Axis Sally, on the Rome radio, put her oar in. "Hello, you brave Americans! This is Sally. By the way, you 36th men, you can sew your T patches back on—we know where you are."

You'll know it worse pretty soon, you bitch, Willie Condett thought. We'll make you know it. From Major General Fred Walker, the short, soft-spoken Ohioan commanding these Texans, down to the lowest private, 36th Division was bitter—and rough.

After dark May 25, the division moved forward to a position west of Cisterna, which had just fallen to the 3rd division. Willie knew the orders had been that the 36th would pass through the weary and shot-up blue-and-white patchers, and take up the attack toward Valmontone. Third Division, which had made the initial attack against prepared positions, had run out of steam. It was having trouble even in reaching Artena.

But it didn't go like that. The orders were changed.

Six Corps was going to attack northwest, into the Colli Laziali. A lot of divisions and units had to be shuffled, and the roads were choked with traffic. For two days, the 36th sat on its duff, waiting.

Meanwhile, Willie heard the 34th Division, the 45th and the 1st Armored, striking along the Lanuvio-Campoleone axis, had run head on into I Parachute Corps, which no one had known was there. And those Kraut paratroops were as tough as any Fifth Army had seen. The attack northwest had hit a brick wall. The march to Rome had bogged down in a circle of futility.

Von Vietinghoff was escaping through Valmontone, and Rome was as far away as ever. Nothing was going right.

On May 27, Willie Condett's battalion received orders to march on Velletri. Somewhere, somehow, VI Corps had to breach the German line. And with axis of attack irrevocably shifted, Velletri was the key to Rome. From it Highway 7 could be cut, and VI Corps could send forces across the Colli Laziali into Rome itself.

But Velletri was a key link in the German Caesar Line, and they had no intention of giving it up. They had already fought the 1st Armored Division to a standstill a couple of miles outside the town.

Swinging to the attack, Condett's 1st Battalion moved forward all May 27 in the approach. Companies were spread out, looking for contact. But this day they found no Germans. They were swinging around to the east of Velletri, through country the Germans had abandoned.

On May 28, again the battalion, keeping contact on either flank, moved forward. There were a few brief skirmishes, and eighteen prisoners were taken. But few Germans were seen.

That night 1st Battalion halted just across Highway 7 east of Velletri. Willie Condett crossed the road, found a culvert, and set up the battalion CP. They were only two and a half miles from Velletri, lying to the west like an ancient jewel in the setting sun. The town was perched high in the Colli Laziali, and behind it rose the dark bulk of Monte Artemisio, bristling with OPs and dug-in 88s. Willie could see that his battalion was going to have to attack down the highway, straight into town, while other outfits of the 36th assaulted along Highway 7 coming in the far side. There was no other way to do it. From the rear, the steep slopes of Monte Artemisio ringed the town, protecting it.

In the foothills, in the vineyards and rock-strewn fields, behind the plastered stone farmhouses, were MG 42s, Panzers, 77-mm. and 88-mm. AT guns, Teller mines, mortars. The slopes over Velletri bristled with heavy gun emplacements. And the weapons were in the hands of tough, unbeaten German veterans.

Armor, artillery and air had all hammered at Velletri for days. But they couldn't take the town. Only dogfaces could do that.

We are going to catch hell, Willie Condett thought, standing in the dusk. *But the Krauts are going to catch it, too.* He quit worrying.

At dark, 1st Battalion stopped where it was, all slung out along Highway 7 south and east of Velletri. Lieutenant Colonel Kilrain, newly assigned as CO of the battalion, listened to Captain Condett's advice: "Colonel, we'd better pull our units back, button up for the night. The way we are now, all strung out, even a patrol could give us trouble by slipping through."

Kilrain, bespectacled and heavy-set, a ruddy-faced man in his early forties, finally agreed. Then, standing to his full five feet eight, he told Condett, "Captain, you have more combat than I have, but remember, I have a lot more training for war than you do. Don't forget that." Kilrain was a regular Army officer.

Somehow, Willie Condett, ex-bus driver, was able to remember that statement quite easily. He never forgot it.

The night passed.

With early dawn, Willie was out with the line companies, checking, co-ordinating, making sure all officers knew the score. Like the nights, the early mornings were cool up here in the Alban Hills, even for wool uniforms and field jackets. But the May days warmed up—especially when the Schnauzer MG 42s barked and snarled.

Around his grimy dogfaces, he found Italian civilians, everywhere. The

Eyeties were out on the roads, now, shouting and waving. They knew the iron German grip on this country was loosening. They held bottles of cool wine, plying the dusty and thirsty troops with Dago red. Willie saw a few of the battalion's men had plied too easily, and he spoke sharply to the officers about it. They weren't going to beat the Kraut paratroopers half-crocked!

"Get out of here—vamoose !" Willie yelled at the laughing, waving Italian farmers. *"Tedeschi!"* He pointed toward Velletri. "Plenty boom-boom around here pretty soon." The girls smiled and waved back at him. Obviously, they didn't understand a word. And just as obviously, the tall, blue-eyed *capitano* could have anything he wanted, too.

Willie gave up and went on. He felt sorry for the poor Dagos. Sure, they had backed Mussolini, asked for what they got. But their whole damn country was being taken apart piece by piece; both Krauts and Americans and British grabbed their women, and everything that wasn't nailed down was being liberated by one army or the other. The Italians could do nothing but live through it, if they could.

At least, however, they preferred the *Americani* to the *Tedeschi.*

With the attack ready to move off, Willie returned to the battalion CP. Inside, he found Lieutenant Colonel Kilrain standing stunned and inarticulate in front of the short, blocky form of General Walker, the division commander.

"Where are your troop dispositions?" the blunt, soft-spoken Ohioan demanded.

Kilrain didn't know. His face was puffy, and he was red-eyed.

"You're relieved of command," Walker said.

An attached light colonel, Ramsay, was placed in command. Then Walker left.

Kilrain looked at Willie desperately. "The Old Man thought I'd been drinking—but I was only asleep when he came in."

Which probably was the truth, Willie thought. Still, as CO, Kilrain should have been alert, known what was going on. Combat, where they used real bullets, was a hell of a lot different from training maneuvers.

Colonel Ramsay took over. A smooth-faced six-footer, in his early thirties, and a West Pointer, Ramsay got things moving fast. He and Willie talked the same language when it came to killing Krauts.

The battalion attacked toward Velletri, with one platoon from Charlie and Able Companies on the right of Highway 7, the bulk of the battalion on the left. Willie went with Charlie Company.

At once, they hit stiff opposition. Kraut fire laced at them from trees, from terraced gardens, from farmhouses. But a battalion of SP guns attacked with them and, strong point by strong point, the enemy positions were reduced. The huge 90-mm, shells blew down whole houses.

Willie, accompanying C Company, reached a rose garden, terraced along a steep slope. Just ahead was a railroad embankment. A storm of small-arms fire tore the earth around him. The Krauts were entrenched behind the embankment, keeping up a deadly fire.

Several of the C Company men were down, bleeding on the dusty ground.

"Bring those damn TDs up," Willie ordered.

But the tank destroyers couldn't cross the embankment; the grade was too steep. While they supported by fire, C Company overran the embankment, pushing the Germans back. Willie, not taking part in the fight, asked the tank destroyer officer to get the TDs up forward, to support the infantry. The country was crawling with Kraut armor.

But they found the TDs couldn't get across the railroad embankment without engineer support. Cursing, Willie left the TDs and plunged after the advancing Charlie Company boys. The only antitank protection they had now were a couple of tiny 57-mm. AT guns, which could be lifted over the grade.

The advance slowed in the thick brush on each side of the road.

As Willie ran to catch up with C Company, a German motorcycle courier buzzed down the highway. The Krauts were mixed up this morning—they weren't sure just where the Americans had crossed Highway 7.

"Shoot him! Shoot him!" Willie shouted. Before he could draw his own 45, a hail of rifle fire knocked the rider down, killed him. Willie pulled back the dead. Kraut's jacket, looked for papers. But whatever dispatches the German youth had carried had been in his head.

Willie rejoined the company, moving along with Tully, the company commander. Lieutenant Tully, a sandy-haired young replacement officer up from the ranks, kept the attack moving. As a staff officer, it wasn't Willie's job to interfere with Tully, or to get in the fight. He was there to co-ordinate, and to ensure that Ramsay's orders were carried out.

All morning, the advance inched forward. The terrain held 1st Battalion back as much as the enemy, for they had not come to the Kraut's main defense line.

Just before noon, a Kraut Mark VI—Tiger—tank clanked up the highway from the direction of Velletri. The Germans wanted to find out if the road was open, apparently. The long, low silhouette hugged the road; the enormously elongated barrel of its 88-mm. gun swung evilly, like the head of a great, black snake. Willie and the around him hugged the ground along the hill slopes.

Pow!

Just below Willie, one of the little 57s fired on the Tiger. It did about as much damage as a pop gun to the thick armor plate of the tank turret. And in their excitement, the gunners had forgotten to remove the 57's camouflage netting before firing. Set afire, it blazed smokily and marked the AT gun's position.

"Oh, my God! Oh, my God!" the gunners screamed, getting the hell away from there.

The Tiger opened fire with its machine guns, spraying the area. First Battalion opened up with small arms, but it couldn't hurt the steel monster without the 90s of the tank destroyers behind the railroad.

Willie grabbed a sergeant by the arm. "Get back—get some artillery fire on this road." He gave the NCO the coordinates. "Tell 'em to fire, even if they drop in on us." There was no other way to handle that damned Tiger. In the open, it could hold up the battalion for hours.

But now, under the hail of small arms fire, the tank was trying to turn around in the road. Finally, it backed away, fleeing toward Velletri. The Kraut tank commander had found out what he wanted to know.

Which was just as well, because the requested artillery support never came.

The attack toward Velletri proceeded, but it was damned slow work. Two and a half miles could be a long way to go.

The morning of May 30, Memorial Day back home, General Fred Walker was trying to sell something to General Truscott, his corps commander. Truscott was not sure it wasn't a bill of goods, at first.

The two generals stood in the 36th's CP, midway between Cisterna and Velletri. Fred Walker insisted that his reconnaissance had just found a gap in the German lines east of Velletri. His engineers were certain troops could pass through this gap to reach the crest of the Colli Laziali behind Velletri. Hell, with a little engineer support, even tanks could make it over the trail. Once on top of Monte Artemisio, the 36th could take the Germans in the rear.

Sure, it was dangerous. If the Germans closed their lines, discovered the Americans trying to infiltrate their rear, it could mean the loss of several thousand men. It could be worse than the Ranger deal at Cisterna.

But Fred Walker had had to order his men to attack frontally into overwhelming German fire on the Rapido. He hadn't like frontal assaults then; he didn't now. Not when there seemed to be a better way to do it.

Truscott wanted to talk with the engineer officer who had made the reconnaissance. That officer backed up everything Walker said. The Germans, hard-pressed, had apparently counted on the steep slopes of the Colli Laziali to bar any American advance along part of their line and had left that part completely undefended.

Up to this time, whenever commanders had stuck out their necks, they had usually gotten them chopped off. But Lucian Truscott, as CG of the 3rd Division, had had an unusual policy: no officer or EM who acted on his own initiative in the absence of orders had ever been punished. The contrary had been division policy—any officer or man who failed to act on his own initiative where strong original action was called for was removed.

"Get on with it," Truscott told Walker. "I'll authorize corps engineers to assist you."

The plan was quickly hammered out. The 36th U.S. Engineers would move in to relieve part of the 36th Division on line; the 142nd Infantry, under Colonel George Lynch, would pass through the 141st Infantry, in whose area the gap lay, then climb the steep, wooded slopes of the Colli Laziali during the night of May 30. The next day, the 143rd would follow. By June 1 both infiltrated regiments would be in position to strike Velletri from the sides and rear, where the Germans thought they were invulnerable. The 141st Infantry, astride Highway 7, would attack frontally into the town.

It was 1600 hours, May 30, when the verbal orders were issued. After that, Fred Walker paced back and forth, speaking to no one in the CP under the railroad trestle.

Inside the shell-splashed and rubble-strewn town of Velletri, *Hauptmann* Georg Krelitz listened to the report of Senior Sergeant Enno Wanda. Wanda's company had heard firing along the slopes of Mount Artemisio, during the night, and it seemed that somehow a few Amis had gotten in back of the town. Not very concerned, Battalion Commander Krelitz; called his regimental CO.

"Probably an American company or two, *Herr Oberst-leutnant.* Nothing larger could come over the mountain."

"Very well, my dear Krelitz," the colonel said. "Why don't you take your battalion and wipe them up after daylight?"

Krelitz, a light-haired, gaunt Prussian, hung up the phone. He turned his pock-marked face back to Wanda, who said, *"Herr Hauptmann,* we do not know if it is only a company. Suppose the Amis are trying to infiltrate?"

Krelitz smiled tiredly, his thin lips a slash in his hard mouth. "My dear Sergeant," he said in a mild voice, "we have both been some time in Italy. Americans are not Rus\sians. Have they ever done anything but rush straight ahead, into our fire?"

Wanda saluted stiffly and went out.

So—a little action after dawn, Krelitz thought. His tough *Fallschirmjäger* could handle anything the Amis had moved over the hills. He picked up a tin of Hamburg herring, listening to some shooting down Highway 7, to the east. In the dim candlelight, he could read an inscription on the tin. *Zum Bier besonders Schmackhaft!* Good with beer.

With a short curse, he threw the herring tin against the stone wall. His nerves were jumping like wires; his aching eyes felt like hot coals. *For day and days we hold here, while the stupid Amis kill themselves. It must end sometime.*

123

He could not know that it was going to end very soon.

At 0300 hours, June 1, Captain Willie Condett, S-3 of 1st Battalion, 141st Infantry, stood on the second story of the stone farmhouse that served as battalion CP. All around the Krauts' heavy mortar fire was crashing in. *Bam! Bam! Bam!*

For two nights, while 1st Battalion held its position along the road, he had helped the 142nd and 143rd Regiments pass down the road and climb the steep slopes of Monte Artemisio, rising like a solid wall of granite to the north. By God, American engineers were wonderful! By now, even tanks and jeeps and trucks were climbing over the Colli Laziali. In a few hours, the Krauts were going to catch it in the ass.

But he had his own outfit to worry about. It was drawing the fun job again. It would advance straight up the road, right into Velletri. Even with the other regiments attacking the Krauts from the rear, it was going to be rough. But with the infiltration, it would be possible. First Battalion had been resupplied, and it had a new Heavy Weapons company attached.

Beside Willie, a machine gun opened up, hammering tracers out into the darkness that shrouded the German lines. First Battalion had already begun to move forward, attacking in the night.

Crash! A German AP shell shrieked in the open window, shattering the opposite wall. *To hell with this noise.* Leaving the shaken gunners, Willie went downstairs, joined Colonel Ramsay.

By daylight, the attack was going fine on the left, or west, side of the highway. But something was loused up on the right. Those platoons had not only failed to keep up; they had pulled back.

The lean, taut Ramsay, blue eyes crackling, snapped at Willie, "Get over there and get them straightened out. Find out who's in charge, and relieve him!"

"Yes, sir," Willie said. From the battalion staff he picked Lieutenant Karam, a steady, dark young Syrian-American. "Come on, Karam, let's go."

The road curved through steep slopes, with tall woods rising from the hillsides. On each side of the road, a man had cover—but the highway itself was open, and from the hills on either side the Krauts had a fine view. As Karam and Willie raced across the paved surface, machine-gun fire hissed at them.

Safely across, Willie panted at the first infantryman he saw, "Who's in charge?" The troops had been stopped by some sort of gravel pit ahead.

"The lieutenant's back there." The grimy, bearded soldiers pointed. The Americans lay huddled in the rocks and trees, while Kraut mortars kept plastering them. In a shallow hole, Willie and Karam found two lieutenants. Willie didn't engage in conversation.

"You're both relieved of command," he said. "Lieutenant Karam's taking

124

over both platoons."

Karam, black eyes steady, took a few minutes to organize both platoons, one from C and one from A, into one unit. Then he formed a solid base of fire, and sent his assault element forward. Under his sharp commands, the dogfaces moved.

Plunging across the gravel pit, they caught several Krauts trying to get away. When the Germans saw the Americans firing at them, they tore off their steel helmets, threw up their hands.

"Hell with taking prisoners," Willie snapped. "We don't want to get cluttered up with 'em while we're trying to advance."

Years later, because Willie Condett was a decent man caught up in war, he would remember this moment and be ashamed. He would not be alone.

With Karam advancing well, he decided to go back across the road to join Ramsay and the command group. He trotted out into the open, looking up to a small knob rising just above him, and he realized he should have looked before he moved onto the road.

Just above him, on the knob, he saw several Krauts in big helmets, swiveling a machine gun to fire at him.

He had only his .45 automatic, and one hand grenade.

Willie drew his pistol, emptying it toward the Germans as he ran. He killed one German. Then Willie, knowing he was a dead duck if he hit the ground, or if he tried to make the brush on either side of the road, charged the machine gun, throwing the single grenade. As he let it go, he hit the dirt, clawing at the ground. His steel helmet bounced away.

The Kraut MG fired, putting two holes in his bouncing helmet. The gunners tried to depress the muzzle to cover him, while Willie watched helplessly. He could hear the Krauts yelling something to each other.

Oh, crap, this is it! he thought, almost calmly.

Then his grenade went off. The Germans screamed and ducked down behind the knob. One of them was hit.

Willie got up. He saw a half-dozen riflemen of C Company running toward him. They had seen Willie pinned down in the road, and they had dashed forward to get the machine gun off his back. They blazed away at the German crew. One of them knew German, and he shouted and cursed at the gun crew as he came on, firing.

The Germans threw up their hands. Two were killed and four captured. Willie waved at the C Company boys, and continued across the road.

Now the tenor of the attack was changing. In Velletri, the Krauts had discovered they were ringed, as the 141st's sister regiments took them in the rear. Their plan changed from stubborn defense to attempts to break out. Inside Velletri, all was confusion—burning houses, smashed vehicles, dead men and horses littering the streets. Velletri had been a German communications hub, and units pulling back from other areas had piled up inside it. Now they were trapped.

Air and artillery blasted at the town, and the 36th Division ground toward it, inexorably. By noon, Willie's battalion had reached the outskirts of Velletri. Fighting was steady, but it was becoming chaotic.

Neither the Germans nor the Americans knew exactly where they were, or where the enemy was. It was hard to keep contact with adjacent units, under the terrible shelling that rained down on both sides. The Krauts were pulling back swiftly now, so that 1st Battalion's advance was uneven.

Willie Condett, moving down the highway into the outskirts of town, could see Germans moving back. They dashed from house to house, and darted across the fields. Beside Willie walked Captain Arn, the Heavy Weapons Company Commander, and Lieutenant Colonel Reese, the Division Inspector General. Just behind them rolled a big tank destroyer, its 90-mm. gun barrel rising over them.

None of them knew it, but they had gotten ahead of the battalion line of advance. As it was, the IG had no business being up front at all, but he told Willie he wanted to get a Kraut or two. He and Captain Arn carried carbines, and they were firing at the Krauts running across the stony fields. The Germans seemed mainly intent on pulling back, rather than standing to fight.

Then, suddenly, around a turn in the road, came the freezing, terrifying sound of a Mark VI. The Tiger clanked around the bend, the long snout of its 88 poking out at the little knot of officers standing naked in the middle of the road.

It was Willie's old friend from back at the railroad embankment, and it was the ugliest sight he had ever seen.

The tank destroyer, thin-skinned and unready to fire, pulled back, leaving Willie, Arn and Reese standing alone. The tank gun spat green-yellow flame, and the shrieking AP shell struck Lieutenant Colonel Hal Reese, eviscerating him. Then the Tiger opened up with its machine gun.

There was a stone building twenty-five feet to Willie's right, and he ran for his life, Arn plunging along behind him. Miraculously, both of them reached the building through the hail of projectiles.

Inside the stone house, Willie crawled on his knees to the window and looked out. The damned tank was swiveling its gun to face the window. He pressed himself against the dusty floor.

The tank fired twice, smashing AP projectiles clear through the wall. Splinters flew and Willie choked on the rising dust. If the Tiger had had HE shells, that would have been it. But the armor-piercing rounds passed through the walls, missing both of the huddled officers.

Arn moaned, his face very pale. "I'm shot," he told Willie.

Willie looked. "The hell you are—I don't see any blood."

126

"Damn it, I'm hit in the ass," Arn snapped. And he was—a bullet had penetrated both cheeks. It was a painful wound. Willie took out his first-aid packet, poured sulfa on Arn's buttocks.

Outside, the tank's engines still roared, but it held its fire. Several Krauts were shouting at the tank. *Telling him to let us have it again, Willie thought. Where the hell are our troops? We must have got far ahead of the battalion advance.*

Willie Condett had been awarded the Silver Star with Oak Leaf Cluster, and the Purple Heart. For his action against the machine gun today, he would receive the Bronze Star. Now, as the tank clanked up closer to the building, he stayed down, hugging the floor with Arn. Any man who fought a Tiger tank with a .45 wasn't brave—he was soon dead.

The P-38 Willie had picked up from a dead German *officer* dug into his side. He had placed it in his belt and forgotten it. Now he pulled the wicked Kraut pistol out and looked about for a place to conceal it. *At the best, we'll be captured,* he thought, and a *"liberated"pistol will give the krauts the red ass for sure—they'll shoot us on the spot.*

He was remembering what he had told the boys of Charlie Company, when the Krauts had tried to surrender at the gravel pit.

He drew his own .45, cocked it and covered the door.

But he never had to use it. There was a crash of rifle fire from the street, the blast of grenades. With a roar, the tank engine revved up, and the horrible sound retreated deeper into the shambles of Velletri.

Looking out the window carefully, Willie saw American infantrymen advancing down the road, firing on the fleeing Krauts.

A minute later, the cheerful, sandy-haired face of Lieutenant Tully poked into the door. Tully grinned at Willie. Tully's boys were making a habit of bailing Willie Condett out. Leaving Arn for the medics, Willie rejoined Charlie Company.

Tully's men pushed slowly ahead, moving around German bodies and the bloated corpses of German artillery horses lying in the streets. When they passed a house, the beareded infantrymen tossed a grenade in the cellar. Why take chances?

Trapped, the Krauts began to surrender now in droves. They came out of houses holding white flags, without helmets, holding only their mess kits. Many of them were wounded. They were defeated, shell-shocked, despondent. Willie organized them into long columns, sending them back to the rear. There was no need to put guards on them—they had had enough.

Later in the afternoon, 1st Battalion was ordered to pull out of Velletri, take up blocking positions on the west. Second Battalion passed through them for the final mop-up. Velletri was taken.

The slaughter on the Rapido had been avenged, many times over. As Willie saw to it that the tired companies took up their positions, a voluble

127

Italian rushed up to the nearest dogfaces. He yelled at them in excited Italian, until someone was found to translate.

"He says he's a doctor, and he's just delivered a *bambino*. Since the Americans have conquered the town, he wants to know if the boy will be an American citizen."

Suddenly, Captain William P. Condett began to laugh. It was the first time he'd really laughed in a long time. He sat down on a curb and laughed and laughed.

Most of the bitterness was gone.

As the sunny afternoon waned, and only scattered shots sounded from the bloody ruin that had been the lovely ancient city of Velletri, General Fred Walker watched General Truscott approach the outskirts of town by jeep.

Walker was still stricken by the news of Hal Reese's death—Reese and he had been close back in the First World War, and long-time friends. Reese, he was thinking, was the finest kind of civilian soldier—a man well into middle age, who had come back into service not because he had to, but because he was needed. *I told him not to get too far ahead out there.*

Now, aloud, he said to Lucian Truscott, "You can go in now, General. The town is yours."

He could have said, "Rome is yours, too." For the last German line of resistance south of Rome was irreparably shattered. At this minute their units were streaming north on Highway 6, to new positions high in the Apennines.

Up ahead, across the Colli Laziali, the Eternal City lay shining and indefensible in the brilliant sunlight. It would bow to American conquerors, as it had bowed to countless others in the past. Velletri had been the key that turned the lock, and if General Key received the key to the city of Rome, it was the 36th Division which had handed it to him.

On June 4, 1944, two days before the Normandy invasion, elements of the 1st Armored Division entered Rome.

The blood-soaked beachhead at Anzio had served its purpose. Its mission was fulfilled. The southern Italian campaign was history.

The End.

128

About the Author

During World War II, the late Fehrenbach served with the US Infantry and Engineers as platoon sergeant with an engineer battalion. He continued his military career in the Korean War, rising from platoon leader to company commander and then to battalion staff officer of the 72nd Tank battalion, 2nd Infantry Division. Prior to his military involvement, a young T. R. Fehrenbach, born in San Benito, Texas, worked as a farmer and the owner of an insurance company. His most enduring work is *Lone Star*, a one-volume history of Texas. In retirement, he wrote a political column for a San Antonio newspaper. He sold numerous pieces to publications such as the *Saturday Evening Post* and *Argosy*. He is author of several books, including *U.S. Marines in Action*, *The Battle of Anzio*, and *This Kind of War*.

OPEN ROAD
INTEGRATED MEDIA

Open Road Integrated Media is a digital publisher and multimedia content company. Open Road creates connections between authors and their audiences by marketing its ebooks through a new proprietary online platform, which uses premium video content and social media.

CPSIA information can be obtained
at www.ICGtesting.com
Printed in the USA
LVOW10s1446260218
567893LV00001B/10/P